PLAY OR DIE

SENIOR TENNIS AND THE ART OF SPIN

Robert J. Ray, Ph.D.

PLAY OR DIE

SENIOR TENNIS AND THE ART OF SPIN

Robert J. Ray, Ph.D.

For David
Intrepid Trimmer of Trees

Thanks,
Dr Ray
Seattle 2023

Copyright © 2023 Robert J Ray

All rights reserved.

No part of this book may be reproduced, stored in a retrieval system, or transmitted in any form or by any means, electronic, mechanical, photocopying, recording, or otherwise, without the express written permission of the author, except for the use of quotations in a book review.

It is important to note that the author is not a professional tennis coach or certified instructor. The information provided in this book is based solely on the author's personal experiences and opinions. Readers are advised to consult with qualified professionals before implementing any techniques or advice mentioned. Names have been changed or abbreviated to protect privacy. The author, publisher, and associated parties shall not be held liable for any consequences arising from the use or misuse of the information provided in this book.

Cover Art by Meredith Bricken Mills
Photo by Paul Haley

ISBN: 978-1-7372178-4-8 (paperback)

First Edition

Made in the United States of America.

*This book is for Margot,
lovely wife, cheerful cheer-leader:
"Swat that ball, Bob."*

CONTENTS

PLAY OR DIE
Title Page
Copyright
Dedication
PART I 1
THE RE-ENTRY OF AN ELDER TENNIS PLAYER 2
GETTING YOURSELF RATED 6
BALL MACHINE 2.5 13
COACH JT AND THE BIRTH OF TCSP 21
THE BUILDING OF THE BUILDING 24
MIXED DOUBLES MIXUP WITH PLAYER Q 30
A LESSON FROM COACH MB 35
THE FINE ART OF SOCIAL EXCLUSION 39
SD&P WITH COACH MB 45
LESTER MAKES A TENNIS FRIEND 51
ON THE COURT WITH COACH MB 53
THE MAN WITH THE NIKE SWOOSH FOREHAND ... 57
TACTICAL TENNIS E-MAILS 63
PART II 68
BODY-WORK: LESTER WARMS UP 69

PEP TALK FROM LESTER	71
THREE OLD TENNIS FRIENDS	73
SMART SHOTS FOR SENIOR DOUBLES	75
PART III	85
HOW TO SURVIVE AND THRIVE IN COMP SENIOR DOUBLES	86
SILENT SMIRKS AND BODY LANGUAGE: ANTICS OF THE A-TEAM	89
INJURED ATHLETE	94
FIVE WOUNDED SENIORS	100
PART IV	110
LESTER'S FIRST A-TEAM	111
LESTER DISCOVERS SPIN IN SPORTS	117
THE DEFINITION OF STATUS	122
MODESTO JUNIOR COLLEGE	125
THE LONG TENNIS SHADOW OF MODESTO JC	135
ESCAPE TO CALIFORNIA	140
SO LONG ICE, GOODBYE SNOW	144
PART V	148
ALL ALONE IN CALIFORNIA	149
TENNIS WITH DENNIS	151
WITH A SMIDGEN OF TENNIS EDUCATION LESTER LANDS A TENNIS JOB	156
HITTING LANES AT THE VIC BRADEN TENNIS COLLEGE	158
IN THE GROOVE WITH ED COLLINS	162
NOONTIME MESSENGER—THE TURBULENT LIFE OF A TENNIS PRO	166
BOUNCE-HIT WITH TIMOTHY GALLWEY	169
DESPERATELY SEEKING THE NEW MRS. LESTER	174

PART VI	178
TEACHING TENNIS AND GETTING OLD	179
LESTER'S LAST TENNIS LESSON	184
THE ART OF DENIAL	187
APPENDIX ONE: THE BYRANT PARK THREESOME	190
SHORT COURT	195
PLAYER JD AND HER CROSS-CULTURAL MUSINGS	197
PLAYER PH AND HIS RHYMES	199
APPENDIX TWO: OF TENNIS, THEY DO SING	201
OBJECTS ARE FARTHER THAN THEY APPEAR: LIGHTNING AMONG THE RECTANGLES	202
POETRY ON THE COURT	205
PLAYING TO THE LIMIT	207
FEARLESS SENIORS TEST THEMSELVES	209
EPILOGUE: TO GET THERE	212
A TENNIS PILGRIM PILGRIMAGE	213
OFF-COURT READING TO ENHANCE YOUR ON-COURT ACTIVITY	221
Giving Thanks	227
About The Author	229
Books By This Author	231

INTRODUCTION

I hit my first tennis ball on the rough gray concrete depression-era courts at Ellwood Park in Amarillo, Texas.

The ball was pale, the same whitish-gray as the courts—and hard to see against the bland concrete surface. The sun was hot. I wore shorts and a T-shirt and a floppy Army Surplus fatigue hat. My tennis shoes were whitish-gray Keds—they slid on the court.

The racket was a Don Budge Autograph—ancient, clumsy, heavy as a war-club, its cheap nylon strings unraveling.

I was sixteen, a wimpy teen.

My opponent/instructor on that first day was a pleasant man named Mike, who married my mother when I was twelve. Both of us were ping-pong players. Both of us hit crazy slices.

Mike was a better slicer. His balls cleared the net. They torqued when they hit the tough whiteish concrete. Today, looking back at that Sunday afternoon, I see evolutionary biology at work: as a rival male for my mother's affection, I was a target in Mike's gunsights. I was dead meat. He brought me out there so he could win.

Not hard to do, against me—the ultra-non-jock. Medium hand-eye talents, clumsy, klutsy, hopeless. Shabby footwork guaranteed.

I hated team sports. I was too slow for track—my foursome always lost the relay race. I was too chicken for basketball/football, bored by baseball as seen from right field, where the jocks always stuck me. I'd been hoping for a breakthrough in tennis, a non-body contact sport—and I remembered that Sunday spring afternoon because I was struck by an epiphany—a shard of sunlight slashing down, carving into the tough concrete court..

Physics and geometry—I saw targets on the court. I saw pathways.

I saw trajectories.

I saw a place to aim the ball.

A diagonal shot, straight at the cross-court corner.

The net was higher at the posts.

Lower in the center, marked by the strap.

If I hit down the line—the distance was 78 feet—I had to elevate the ball or it would not clear the net—six inches higher, marking the singles sideline.

But if I hit cross-court—the distance for singles was 82.5 feet—then my shot had more travel-room.

So I aimed the ball cross-court, going for the corner created by the meeting of baseline and faded singles sideline—using the net strap as my sighting device—the ball cleared the net (six inches lower at the strap), touching down in front of the baseline, pushing my instructor/opponent back, winning the point for my side—a thrill raced through me, and that shot has been with me ever since.

I didn't win many points on the sunny spring Sunday in Ellwood Park. But tennis is a sport where you keep on learning.

Lessons.
Workouts.
Drills.
Matches.
Reading books and watching the Tennis Channel.

❈ ❈ ❈

The first tennis book I read was *Match Play and the Spin of the Ball*, by Big Bill Tilden, who shows the beginner how to see the tennis ball:

> *"Every ball has an outside and inside edge every time it comes to you...and the edge you hit determines the curve and spin of the ball on your return."*

And I didn't know it that first day, but my first real tennis shot was an inside-out forehand. As a clumsy teen, I did not know the technical term—<u>inside-out-forehand</u>—but I was overjoyed, driving that pale rotating orb across the net, riding the ball, feeling it settle just where the baseline meets the singles alley, not knowing back then that there was even more room in doubles.

I'm still hitting that inside-out forehand decades later. I am eons older, but the court dimensions are the same—and change is on my side:

- The greenish-blue court surface at Tennis Center Sandpoint in Seattle gives me a good look at the oncoming ball.
- The balls today are yellow-green, easier to see than the pale 1950's-era white.
- My racket, a Wilson Ultra 10, strung with Nxt Power 18g filament, gives an old man more feel and a fatter sweet spot.

❈ ❈ ❈

These days, when I hit the inside-out forehand as an elderly oldster, my racket strings brush sideways from right to left, across the back of the ball. My racket face is tilted back—the technical term is open-face—but not open by much. I use the Continental grip, but other hitters of this shot prefer the Eastern. Don't get me wrong. The Inside-Out forehand is not a replacement for the Modern Forehand—the weapon of pros and players who were lucky enough to grow up playing with composites—but it does give an old person another chance.

And more accuracy.

Like other elders, I play tennis to keep from dying. Playing forces me to move. Moving hurts, forcing me to get help from trainers and doctors. Trainers give me exercises to sharpen my play, to keep me on the court longer. Doctors give me shots (Cortisone, Visco Supplementation) that ease the pain in my arthritic knees. Playing has helped me make friends.

I wrote this book for those tennis friends.

PART I

THE RE-ENTRY OF AN ELDER TENNIS PLAYER

A cold bleak day, Soundview Park in Seattle. Lester Elder and his writing buddy, Player ZH, a brother leftie. They're hitting short court, chipping the ball close to the net strap, feet shuffling on winter-chill asphalt.

Lester Elder has bad knees.

He hobbles to the ball.

A blade of yellow sunlight cuts through the grey winter chill, January in Seattle, rain on the way, and then maybe snow.

Lester feels weird, trying to locate his old tennis rhythm.

He misses three shots in a row. Player ZH suggests a solution, the double bounce, giving Lester another couple seconds.

Ten years, maybe fifteen, since Lester has tried to hit a tennis ball.

His knees pump like rusty pistons.

His ankle hurts.

He stumbles, almost falls.

Lester is 79. His buddy, Player ZH, is 68.

Short court means staying inside the service boxes. Hitting soft, with spin.

Jagged sunlight through the trees. Lester misses four in a

row. He asks about group lessons—Player ZH works out at Amy Yee—he tells Lester about the rating system, courtesy of the USTA. Player ZH is a 3.0. Lester is lower than that. Way lower.

Lester nails three in a row, boom, boom-boom. The double-bounce technique is working. As he moves, Lester feels warmer. Warm enough to try more slice. Big deal, the ball nicks the tape and dies. His ankle twists. The sudden imbalance shoots a pain up the fibula to Lester's knee. He sits on a soggy bench, feeling betrayed. Player ZH points out Lester's track shoes. Not good for tennis, he says. Track shoes go forward. Tennis shoes go sideways.

Lester bumps fists with Player ZH.

Thanks for the hit. For getting me out there.

No problem, bro.

* * *

Lester limps back to his car. Where are those old tennis shoes? His house is two short blocks and three corner turns away from the courts in this curved street neighborhood in Seattle. He parks the car and limps to the front door. He's lying in bed watching the Tennis Channel when Mrs. Lester appears, checking on him.

How did the re-entry go?

Great, he says. We let the ball bounce twice.

Is that legal?

Gotta start somewhere.

What's with the ice-pack?

Little twist in the ankle.

How do you feel about today, getting back into it, I mean?

Gotta take some lessons, he says.

There's that place in Magnuson Park, she says.

What's the name, do you know?

Magnuson, I think.

Local hero, right?

Norwegian Viking Swede, she says. That's the legend.

There's also a new-fangled ratings system, Lester says. Courtesy of our power-brokers in the USTA.

How long has it been, not playing?

Maybe fifteen years.

And you still love it, right?

I did today.

Even with the ankle?

Yeah, Lester says. Even with the ankle—have you seen my old tennis shoes?

❋ ❋ ❋

Winter slid into spring. Sudden spring rains kept them off the court, the summer flew by. His friend Player ZH invited him for a doubles match, but Lester said no. The idea of teaming up and losing brought on the shakes—Lester was having trouble facing the obvious reality of old age—his stiffness, his diminished skill level. Did he have any hand-eye coordination left?

On a rainy day in October, Lester joined the Magnuson Tennis Center, two grayish hump-back buildings connected by a gusty breezeway in Magnuson Park—ten indoor courts, with superb lighting and a surface like Laykold, blue with a green background.

The friendly helpers at the Front Desk gave Lester the senior rate, a one-year membership for less than a hundred dollars. Since Lester looked old and lost and bewildered, the Front Desk helpers advised him to get rated. See where he was on the new-fangled USTA rating system—a must when you registered for a class.

The lowest rating number—1.0—designated the absolute beginner, too far down for Lester's ego—he felt fitful, chastised, brushed aside—no question he was better than 1.0. Tennis teams. Tournament experience. Tennis schools, tennis teaching.

Lester Elder was not a lowly beginner.

The top USTA rating, 7.0, was for designated pros who earned money playing tennis (not super-stars, like Federer and Nadal)—something Lester had dreamed about as a teen-ager—big-time sun-tanned tennis in Monte Carlo, tennis on the grass at Wimbledon, tennis on the red clay at Roland Garros. But the harsh unreachable height of 7.0 humbled him. Made him aware—he was Old.

In his two-decade absence, tennis had changed.

Where did Lester belong?

Could he get going again?

Were there any tennis players out there old enough to play with him?

He saw himself—an old man hitting against a wall.

The old man misses. He trudges after the ball. He stoops to pick up the ball.

    Fade out.

GETTING YOURSELF RATED

Lester's Ratings Class took place on Courts 1 and 2 in the main building at Magnuson Tennis Center, where he was the oldest person standing askew and hurting on the smooth blue-green indoor turf.

Lester counted 27 tennis players signed up to be tested. Half looked super-young—athletes bursting with energy and confidence, smooth muscles rippling.

The leftovers looked older—50's or 60's. A woman in a puce track suit gave Lester a nervous smile, then looked away. At 79, grey and stooped and nervous, Lester was the oldest guy getting rated. He felt weird, out of place. Alone on an ancient island of gritty senescence. Feeling isolated from the herd. Had he ever been young enough to bound around the court? Were these young athletes rated 3.5? Or maybe 4.0?

The pro in charge of the ratings class was Coach DD, a solid-looking guy exuding confidence and authority, wearing a sharp track suit and pricey tennis shoes. Coach DD started with a quick lecture on the difference between court shoes and trail shoes. The same message from Player ZH—but Lester hadn't listened.

Trail shoes, said Coach DD, are for moving forward—walking or running straight ahead.

Court shoes, on the other hand, are for moving sideways. If you play tennis in trail shoes, you will fall. You will twist an ankle or a knee. You will suffer untold injuries.

As he finished his pep-talk, Coach DD looked at Lester —first his face, then his feet. Oops. Lester was wearing trail shoes. He felt trapped—not a good way to get yourself rated, wearing the wrong shoes. Why hadn't he listened to Player ZH? Why hadn't he bought some new tennis shoes?

One good reason: Back there at the dawn of his comeback, Lester hadn't needed to move on the court. He only hit short-court. He was taking it slow on purpose, careful not to pop a knee, sprain an ankle. And the trail shoes were in his closet. Easy to find. And back then Lester didn't know whether or not he could still hit the ball. For almost two decades, he hadn't needed any real tennis shoes.

Coach DD smiled—came to the rescue, his eye on Lester's feet—trail shoes were okay for the ratings class. Then he held up a racket with a large oversize face and an ever-widening string-bed that was widest at the top of the frame. If you're a senior player, said Coach DD, this is the racket for you. The sweet spot is larger. It's perfect for seniors.

Coach DD looked at Lester. The look said: You are a bona fide Senior, buddy. And you need this stick.

Before he started the testing, Coach DD split the group, sending the sleek young feisty muscular folks over to Court Two. They galloped over, leaping like antelopes, flashing their youthful bounce.

Coach DD had two assistants. Two youngish females in track suits, both clutching clipboards. He sent one assistant to rate the young people, the designated A-Team for the day. Lester felt envious. In the old days, with his shots, his tennis brain, he would have been over there.

Coach DD divided Lester's group into two lines. Players on the right hit forehands. Players on the left hit backhands. Since Lester was a Leftie, he would work his forehand when the other players hit backhands. He had a plan. When everyone in his line hit middle-range forehands, Lester would let go with his backhand slice. Not showing off, just getting the job done.

Lester was not ready when Coach DD dribbled the ball his way.

It landed way too short.

Forcing Lester to move forward.

He hadn't been training with a one-bounce ball.

He'd been practicing with Player ZH hitting the ball on the second bounce.

He fluffed the first two backhands—into the net.

Coach DD gave him his coach look.

Four more balls to go and Lester was sweating.

Coach DD dribbled ball three. It came in low and slow. But to Lester's eye, it was sudden. Super-fast, dying as it dropped to the court. His brain froze. What was he doing here? You can do it, said Coach DD. Lester reached the next ball before it sank. His backhand slice had always been his money-shot. Lester's stroke started with the racket above the right shoulder. Both hands on the stick. In the ratings class, facing Coach DD, stumbling toward the oncoming ball, Lester's brain froze.

And the world of tennis went out of focus. He had hit this shot a million times. The racket sliced down, catching the ball on the tip of the frame, sending it spinning off to the side, into the net that separated Courts 1 and 2.

And while Lester was dying because of his lousy backhand, here came ball four. Shaken by his lack of control, Lester drove ball four into the net. Balls five and six, he bumped over. Sloppy contact and no follow through. He saw sadness in the eyes of Coach DD. Or was it disdain? What was Lester doing here?

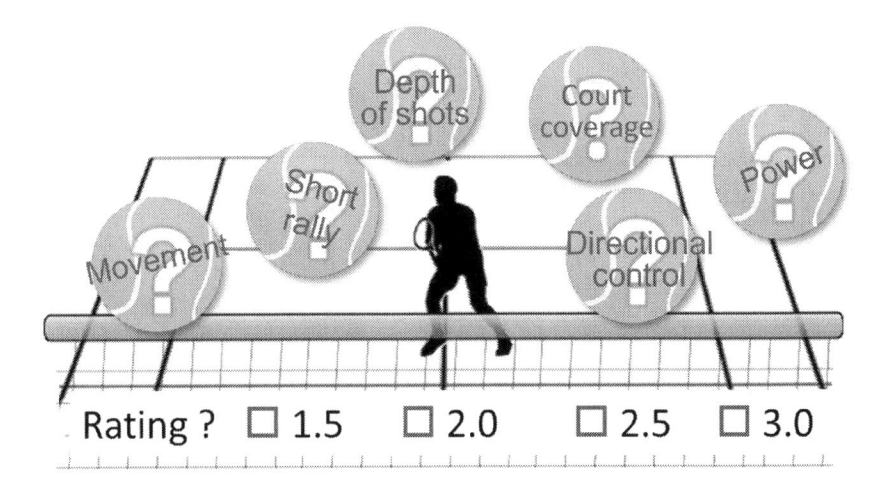

Depth of shots *Court coverage* *Short rally* *Movement* *Directional control* *Power*

Rating ?   ☐ 1.5   ☐ 2.0   ☐ 2.5   ☐ 3.0

On shaky legs, Lester rotated to the back of the other line, backhands for right-handers, for Lester, the suspect lefty forehand. A straight no-nonsense back-swing, the racket face tilted back, open just a hair for the tricky flat forehand. For Lefties, the forehand was deceptive, the money shot.

The woman in front of Lester turned to him and said, I'm really nervous.

Me, too, Lester said.

Are you just starting out? she said.

Yeah, Lester said. Hoping to get a class.

I like ball machine, the woman said.

Sounds good, Lester said.

I'm Lou-Ann, the woman said.

I'm Lester.

He was going to say more—talking calmed his nerves—but it was Lou-Ann's turn to hit backhands. He watched her fumble the ball and felt better. But her fumble didn't help Lester display his subtle untested Fabrice Santoro forehand. Because just as he made contact with ball number six, Lester looked up, took his eye off the ball, and peered into his future.

Where he observed Coach DD whispering to the clipboard girl, who was writing on her clipboard. Lester's heart slid sideways.

His peek into the future showed Lester the truth.
They were talking about Lester, deciding his fate.
He was being rated.
His forehand had lost its cool.
He hit a slap-shot.
It zoomed off his strings.
Wobbled in the air.
Hit the tape.
Lost its spin.
And died.
The Ratings Class was over.

Lester shook hands with Coach DD. He asked the price on the fancy racket strung for seniors. Lester was a thrifty guy. He hadn't bought a new racket in two decades. The price for the fancy racket, a Wilson, was $350, discounted because Lester was a club member. Stunned by the price (his last racket purchase, a metal Prince, had cost $49.50). Lester said he'd think about it. Coach DD said the club had a good deal on tennis shoes. When Lester asked—with fear in his throat—about his rating, Coach DD told him to check at the Front Desk.

There was still time left on the court. The younger people started hitting—what else could they do on a rainy day in Seattle?

They did not invite Lester.

Lester checked with the Front Desk. His rating was a lowly 2.0.

❉ ❉ ❉

Lester was pissed. Not because of his bad showing. Not because he had re-trained with Player ZH, taking the ball on the second bounce. Not because Coach DD had seemed to torpedo his audition, his triumphal re-entry into the game he loved. Not because of his 2.0 rating, when he thought he was at least a 3.0. He wanted to protest his rating. But the Front Desk people were not the problem.

The problem was the court

The problem was the surface.

The problem was the lighting (too bright), the net (too high), the dummies he was in line with, the youngish muscular show-off hotshots on Court 2.

The problem was with the official tester—Coach DD.

Lester felt misunderstood. Ambushed by the system.

Driving away from the club, Lester admitted he had made a mistake. The game of tennis was no longer available to him. He was too old. With his bad knees, he would never work his way back to where he was when he gave up the game, 17 years ago.

* * *

Safe back in his house, Lester went to the USTA website and checked the 2.0 rating. Here's what he found at 2.0.

Player 2.0:

Needs on-court experience.

Has obvious stroke weaknesses

but is familiar with basic positions

for singles and doubles play.

Ouch.

The 2.0 rating made Lester feel like a dummy. A klutz. A total loser.

He needed someone to blame. Okay, he blamed the Coach. He blamed his new club. He blamed the USTA. He felt old. He felt like an old fool. He went to bed that night vowing he would never set foot on another tennis court. He confessed his sadness to his wife. She gave him a hug. It's okay, honey.

The next morning Lester watched a tennis match on television. The strokes. The footwork. The arc of the ball. Fell in love all over again. On Monday he phoned the Front Desk and signed up for Ball Machine. There was no 2.0 class. But the pleasant Front Desk helper signed him up for 2.5. He hadn't hit the ball well enough to impress Coach DD. Maybe hitting against a mindless machine would bounce him up to 2.5.

Lester smiled. He was already feeling better.

BALL MACHINE 2.5

Lester's Ball Machine class took place on Court 2, the site of his ignominious downfall a week ago in front of the entire ratings class. The mentor was Coach JT.

Trim. Athletic. Short haircut, shrewd eyes.

And looking all-business in a black track suit.

Eight people in the Ball Machine class.

Four women and four men. The women were thirties and forties, sleek hair-dos—two had the look of affluence. The other two huddled together like sisters.

One of the men was a hotshot—muscular, a mane of blond hair going silver—he bounded across the court, showing off, making macho moves on every ball.

Lester named him Florian.

Florian's buddy was short, blonde going gray, with careful controlled shots that showed tennis lessons buried in his past.

Lester named him Dorian.

Florian, a super self-aware badminton champ, showbiz teeth, calves writhing with muscle, displayed real power. When he hit the ball, it went pop—like you could hear on the Tennis Channel watching the pros in some empty indoor arena east of Uzbekistan. With his muscles and hair, Florian was the preselected status-figure Alpha Male for Lester's Ball Machine class. Eight weeks with this guy?

Coach JT launched Day One of Ball Machine by asking for information: your name, your tennis history, and your favorite tennis shot. He did not ask for your age.

Overhead smash, said Florian.

An echo from Dorian—the overhead, yeah, he said.

Four players chose the forehand as their favorite shot. A woman in a pink tennis outfit said her favorite was the two-fisted backhand. Lester came last.

The lob, he said. Partnered with the drop shot.

And Coach JT gave him a chuckle. An almost-wink.

Because of Coach JT's response, Ball Machine was looking better than the Ratings Class. Not as much pressure to impress. Good energy. A class that held out hope for improvement. And although Lester had played tennis starting in high school, he might even learn something.

Before he fired up the ball machine, Coach JT demonstrated the steps involved in hitting the Modern Forehand, a shot made possible by the new composite rackets, laced with Boron and Titanium.

The grip was a semi-western.

The ready position called for both hands on the racket.

Knees bent, feet apart.

In slow-motion, Coach JT demoed the unit turn.

The short backswing.

The hit, the fan-like rotation of the racket head.

The wrap-around follow-through, catching the racket with your other hand.

Using a remote device, Coach JT started the machine.

A coughing noise, and the machine burped out a ball.

Coach JT's moves looked effortless—total ergonomic precision.

Four quick steps, like Kenny Rosewall getting into position.

Watching Coach JT, Lester saw much to admire.

He was smooth.

He was graceful.

His move to the ball was precise.

The sideways stance, knees bent, weight on both feet—the stance pulsated with efficiency.

His small-loop backswing traced a perfect arc.

Coach JT's unit turn was compact, natural, practiced, no strain, and loaded with torque. The sound of the strings on the ball whispered like a kiss. There was a professional pop and the ball left his strings.

Cleared the net by four feet, and dropped down two feet inside the baseline.

Lester was impressed. The way Coach JT taught, the techniques he used, made the Modern Forehand look doable. Lester had been watching pros hit variations of the Modern Forehand on TV—not only the men, but also the women—these players who played for their lives, their livelihood, their quest for fame, smacking the ball with these new super-compound rackets.

Lester stared at his racket, an old metal Prince. Unwieldy, unbalanced, impossible for the new game. Make a note: buy a new racket.

Like the Ratings Class, Ball Machine took up courts 1 and 2. Machines at the south end. Hitters at the north end. Like a gaggle of cave men, the four guys moved to Court Two. The women clustered together on Court One. The drill was Hit and Recover—designed to keep the players moving.

1. You move to the ball.
2. You hit that ball.
3. Before the next hit, you tag up, making sure to touch your toe to the flat purple plastic disc.

Tagging up rattled Lester's knees. Three shots and Lester felt the fog of fatigue. He was old. The class was young. This pace would kill him.

So he cheated on the tagging-up. He hit five lefty backhands, then rotated out, moving behind the hitters to follow Florian on the backhand line, where he would hit forehands.

Lester gave up trying to tag up.

His toe hurt.

He felt slow.

He felt bitter.

As the obvious leader of the Man-Pack, Florian played the role of a prince. Because of his muscles, the racket in his fist looked light as a badminton bat. When Florian walloped the ball, his blondish iron-grey hair lit up, highlighting the definition in his biceps and triceps. When Florian made contact, the ball exploded.

Dorian, the older shorter lesser incarnation of Florian, claimed he was just starting out. But Lester could see the guy had talent, good hand-eye coordination. As Dorian struck the ball, his eyes were glazed over, a religious experience.

The fourth male in Ball Machine was Player Q. As he waded in after Dorian, Player Q looked closer to Lester's age—maybe only ten years younger. He had quick hands and a killer instinct, which allowed him to hit a nice-looking hardball. Because of his age, Player Q and Lester were brothers of the wasted knee-joint.

Targets.

The assumed targets for the ball-machine hitters were the deep corners of the singles court.

The assumption here was that you still played singles. All the hitters were aiming their balls cross-court.

Except for Lester.

So when his turn came, he kept the ball low, dropping the ball onto the imaginary left toe of the oncoming enemy doubles player. Next shot: Aim down the line.

To Lester, singles was a dim memory of himself at 55—just before he twisted his knee and took a lengthy layoff.

But here he was, playing inside, safe from the wind and rain. The courts were beautiful, the club seethed with magic. Lester was back. How would he survive?

❋ ❋ ❋

Florian was calling to him.

Your turn, buddy!

When he hit his five forehands, Lester compared himself to his three tennis compatriots. He lacked the power of mighty Florian. He lacked the timing of Dorian. He was slower than Player Q, but Lester had better strokes.

Lester's right knee buckled with the sudden weight of moving—his turn to hit.

On the first ball, he missed—no contact.

On the second ball, his strings made contact, but the ball smacked the tape.

Lester felt himself tilting, ready to fall.

He got the next three balls over the net.

Then he got muscled out of the way by Florian the Glorious, who ordered him back to the forehand line—backhand for lefties —where Lester missed the first two backhands.

Had he forgotten that too?

On the way back to tag the orchid disc, Lester devised a survival strategy.

His goal was to get through the next 45 minutes without falling.

If he put less weight on the knee.

If he used shorter steps to approach the ball.

If he started earlier.

If he stayed calm.

If he kept his cool.

If he evaded the panic of failing in public—because Lester was closer to death than anyone on this court—then maybe he would survive his first ball machine class at the TCSP.

Maybe he would feel better.

Feel alive.

Not dead.

Time for Lester to check with Coach JT.

What about the multiple mis-hits, Coach?

Why did Lester keep missing when it was only practice against a machine?

The Coach asked Lester to show him his grip.

Lester heard the low hum of truth.

He blushed.

He hesitated to check his grip.

No way was it the grip. No way.

But then he checked the grip again.

Trapped in the strait-jacket of senior panic, Lester had reverted to the Continental Grip, reaching back to his wood racket days. He had used the same racket wielded by Don Budge to capture two Grand Slams—the Don Budge Autograph from Wilson.

Lester had owned one of those.

Followed by Rod Laver's Dunlop Maxply—Lester had owned three of those babies, hoping for a transfusion of magic from a fellow leftie, Aussie Rod Laver. Where were those Maxplies now?

The specter of Imminent Change stared Lester in the face.

The rackets had changed.

Lester had stayed the same.

The new metals—boron, graphite, titanium—made the Modern Forehand possible.

To hit a Modern Forehand, you needed the Eastern forehand grip—or maybe the semi-Western.

Lester remembered hearing that advice, but he was reverting to his old ways. He was denying the passage of time. Trying to stay young. Trying to reshape his future as an old person playing tennis using the tools of the Old Person when he was younger.

He confessed to the Coach: he didn't have time to switch from the Continental to the Semi-Western.

You'll get it, said Coach JT.

At the 45-minute marker, Coach JT demonstrated the volley, starting with the Ready Position, feet apart, knees bent, both hands on the racket, the racket head at chest-level. With each perfect volley, the Coach moved closer to the net. Made it look easy. The first easy thing today. Lester had read the books. This was not his first lesson.

He knew about the Ready Position. In his 40[s], could still move, he had tipped other players off abou[t] Position. Now here he was, getting tipped off by Coa[ch]

Lester's brain fuddled into a fog. He felt that old creeping sensation. Was that another attempt at Old Fart Superiority in a world crowded with youngish muscled morons? After paying money to take the Ball Machine class, was Lester's smugness turning him stupid on the tennis court?

Still clinging to the illusion that all tennis players could still play singles (even crippled seniors)—the class volleyed hard down the middle.

※ ※ ※

Because he had said goodbye to singles play, Lester hit short angles. Two into the doubles alley. Two short drop-volleys into the service court. Two volleys aimed at the service court T.

As he rotated out of the line, the Coach said, Hey Lester, looks like you've played this game before.

Lester's brain clicked. His fatigue lifted. His knees felt young again. With one sentence, Coach JT had made Lester feel like he was not gonna die today.

The last drill was lobs and overheads—Lester's major weakness—because when he looked up, he got dizzy. But the lob-overhead drill was great for Florian and Dorian—another chance to show off.

A metallic coughing sound came from the ball machine, launching the orb into the air, tough to see up there, the pale white ball against the pale white ceiling. Lester missed the first two. Hit the third one on the frame. Slapped the fourth lob into the net.

Lester had one more ball coming.

He gritted his teeth, fought the cosmic swirl of mainline vertigo, heard the coughing burp of the ball machine, looked up, remembered his early days, when he could still jump, when

...e hit the ball and called out the clock face number—a trick he'd learned at an Inner Game clinic, developed by Timothy Gallwey, a tennis guru from the sixties, the old clock face trick, forcing the deft eye of Self One to communicate to the flailing corpus of Self Two, the two selves working together to nail that ball and creating in their union the perfect overhead smash—which no one noticed except Lester because the whole class and the watchers looking down from the mezzanine, holding their coffee cups, watching the overhead drill from behind the short plexiglas wall—the spectator eyes at that moment were not watching Lester.

* * *

Instead they were watching the thrilling, heart-stopping leap of Florian the Magnificent, taking up the hitting lane beside Lester, playing to the crowd, hanging in the air like Batman, his warrior-smile enforcing the obvious loveliness emanating from his white mane, as the hair deepened the glow of his yacht captain tan.

After cracking the jump-overhead smash, Florian floated back to earth.

Applause from the watchers.

Lester's ball went in—finally.

But the class was over.

Lester shook hands with Coach JT.

Thanked him for a great lesson.

See you next week.

And the Coach said: Welcome to the new game of tennis, Lester.

COACH JT AND THE BIRTH OF TCSP

Coach JT was Lester's first teacher at TCSP. Lester was a newbie. And what he didn't know was that Coach JT was also a founder of TCSP—and also the manager—the guy who hired and fired, the guy who oversaw the classes.

Lester invited Coach JT to lunch. And there he learned about Coach JT's early life, not only playing tennis, but also working for his dad in construction.

That first day in Ball Machine, when Coach JT went out of his way to make Lester feel at home—that gesture triggered Lester's curiosity not only about how the tennis center operated, but how it had come to be—and Coach JT was a big part of that. So Lester asked Coach JT for an interview:

Q&A WITH COACH JT—
OWNER, MANAGER, INTREPID ENTREPRENEUR

Q: When did you start playing tennis?

A: I first started playing tennis in 1987 with my dad. I was horrible so I started my first lesson in 9th grade, and I was 13 years old.

Q: Who was your first tennis teacher?

A: My first coach was a guy by the name of Jim Garley. He was about as charismatic as they come.

Q: How old were you when you played your first tournament?

A: I played my first competitive match in high school for the tennis team, and it was atrocious. I was thrashed 6-0 6-0.

Q: How did you rate yourself against other players your age?

A: I was at the bottom of the barrel. I looked up to the older players as inspiration and wondered how they got that good.

Q: Which tennis shot was hardest to master?

A: The service return. This was never practiced.

Q: Did you play college tennis-team tennis?

A: Didn't play much in college. Had fun with the Husky club a few times but that was about all.

Q: Did you envision yourself playing the tennis circuit?

A: Ha-ha – at no time did I ever have illusions of grandeur of playing anything high-level.

Q: When did you start teaching tennis?

A: I started tinkering with coaching in 2005. It was something fun to do with a few people I knew.

Q: What was your first career choice when you were in college?

A: I had part-time jobs working for a radio station and property management companies in college.

I didn't have any inclination to do construction.

I thought about law school, but I realized pretty quickly that I was done with school after undergraduate studies.

Q: What led you to join the effort at TCSP?

A: The lack of courts quite frankly. The City of Seattle has not done a good job of addressing its growth with the proper number of recreational resources. Tennis was severely underserved (no pun intended).

Q: What was the most interesting thing about building TCSP?

A: Probably the overwhelming support for the project. We knew there would be demand but as we got closer to opening our doors, the demand swelled much bigger than we anticipated.
Also doing a public private partnership with a city like Seattle

was pretty educating. An interesting adventure because it gave me perspective on city processes.

Q: What's your favorite event at TCSP?

A: We don't do many events so I would have to say one of my favorites has been to have members come out and watch our coaches have fun on the courts.

Our opening celebration gala was pretty fun—an evening cocktail dinner party with a pro exhibition, an a capella group singing, and everyone dancing.

THE BUILDING OF THE BUILDING

Lester's favorite entry to TCSP is east on NE 65th street across Sand Point Way NE, heading east into the sun until he turns left on Sportsfield Drive NE, one easy curve, a soccer field on his right, apartments on his left and the building rises up.

Light as the morning air.

Lester parks. He locks the car. He says hello and good morning to the Front Desk. He takes the stairs to the mezzanine. Willy's Café is starting to open. Courts one and two are ball machine. Court three is SD&P, Senior Drill and Play.

Standing on the edge of the mezzanine, Lester looked up. He was curious about this indoor tennis cathedral. How old was it? What was it made of—that bright, white well-lit interior? He stopped. He looked up.

The ceiling was a soft white fabric. Clever efficient light fixtures bounced light off the ceiling. If you looked up to track an enemy lob, you would not lose the ball in a down-facing glare of lights. Lester was impressed. He remembered looking up at the ceiling of the Notre Dame Cathedral, a trip to Paris where he and Mrs. Lester had spent six weeks at L'Alliance Française, struggling their way through French 101.

The Notre Dame cathedral ceiling was stone and weighty wood—enough weight to buckle the walls. The builders solved that problem—and made architectural history—with the flying buttress, which transferred the dead weight of stone to the ground.

The other device was the truss.

For rebuilding the Notre Dame roof after the 2019 fire, carpenters using medieval hand tools built a roof-truss that was three stories tall. Too tall for a cathedral dedicated to tennis—even though you did need enough height for those senior lobs—so Lester took the time to explore both buildings at the TCSP. He started with Building One.

Six courts. One and Two in the East Wing, separated from three, four, five and six by the mezzanine: the Front Desk, Pro Shop, elevator, women's and men's, front stairway and back stairs.

On the mezzanine: offices, staff meeting room, tables, chairs, and Willy's Café.

To sit and view a lesson or a group of league foursomes, you grab a coffee from Willy's—parked between Courts 2 and 3 on the mezzanine—and relax.

Computer research on Google gave Lester snatches of Sand Point history. The history started with wildlife—they were here first.

Beaver. Fish. Deer.

The Native Americans were here next.

Duwamish. Muckleshoot.

Then airplanes, since the flat, open land beside the lake made a
perfect airfield.

Young Navy pilots learned to fly here from the 1920s through the
post-WWII years.

But the most bronze-plaque-worthy aviation event at Sand Point
was the first aerial circumnavigation of the world. In 1924 four Douglas
pontoon biplanes of the US Army Air Service took off for Alaska

and
points west. The 175-day journey took them around the world and back
to Sand Point.

Just maybe that historic achievement bears a slight resemblance to
the "journey" of any aging tennis player trying to return to the court.

Only three planes made it back after suffering multiple crashes,
mechanical failures, and parts replacements.

The Navy pulled out in 1970.

That's when the local squabbling started.

Groups wanted access: Dog walkers. Soccer players. Baseball hero wannabes. Kite flyers. Advocates for the homeless. Aviation advocates who envisioned a handy landing strip, harking back to those Navy Days. The Muckleshoot tribe, invoking ancient fishing rights.

A name took hold: Sand Point Park.

A second name surfaced: Warren G. Magnuson Park.

And still no tennis facility.

With pushes from Skip Norton and the tennis community, hope sprang up for an indoor tennis cathedral.

The first plans for this facility were drawn up by Mel Streeter, local architect and big-time basketball player. Streeter offered free lessons to young children on the courts at Lower Woodland.

The City of Seattle wanted a tennis facility. But what kind?

There were four indoor courts crammed into Hangar 30—across the street from Building no. 2—dating back to Navy days.

Here's Player LC, remembering those days hitting the tennis ball in Hangar 30:

> You entered the Hangar from a small door on the North end of the building. Inside was a creative use of big space, great natural lighting

due to the span of paned windows on either end and with many broken or missing, the ventilation was excellent—even on hot June afternoons.

There was no front desk....there might have been a card table with a pen and some scratch paper. I only had a phone number and the name Coach JT written on it and as far as I knew, word of mouth was the only exposure and an answering machine was the only method of signing up for lessons. I was left with the notion that one could improve—at any age—with solid instruction and desire.

Architect Streeter's plan for a tennis cathedral-pavilion called for an inflated bubble, kept afloat by pump-compressors. Problems here with noise and pump-pollution—exhaust sanctified by the clean sport of tennis flung into the soft moist air of the Pacific Northwest—is still pollution-heavy.
 But the groundwork had been laid.
 The city wanted a tennis facility.
 Rain. Sleet. Snow. Escape to the inside.
 Enter Coach JT and Scott Marshall.
 Coach JT had grown up working construction for his dad. He knew hammers, saws, nails, backhoes—his business was building single custom family homes. He also taught tennis at Hangar 30.
 Marshall was the CEO of Chinook Forest Partners—a forest management firm. He brought financial savvy to the project.
 Coach JT and Marshall got together with Jake Moe (inventive tennis coach and visionary entrepreneur).
 The original founding fathers of TCSP.
 But what structure would replace the idea of the bubble?
 Brick and mortar was too expensive.
 Too much weight in the roof.
 Notre Dame took 188 years to finish.
 The founders of TCSP did not have that long.

When you build a building, you want it to stay standing. If you were building a cathedral in 12th century France, you would use the materials at hand—stone, brick, mortar, wood—supported by flying buttresses and giant trusses.

The building in Magnuson Park needed trusses, but smaller—and lighter in weight.

The founders settled on a fabric roof developed by Accu-Steel, headquarters in Audubon, Iowa. The steel of the frame is hot-dipped galvanized—a process that eliminates rust, slows down deterioration.

The fabric roof cover is a network of polyethylene panels welded together—no Elmer's glue above your head when you swat that ball.

Compared to the stone roof of Notre Dame, the TCSP roof is feather-light.

What's needed to erect a tennis cathedral?

A plot of land—the sandy dirt at Sand Point.

A tennis-playing community.

Expert citizen-managers to keep things moving.

A modern, simplified building plan.

Start with a fabric roof—goodbye lumber, goodbye stone, goodbye
asphalt shingles, goodbye metal roofing and stone-coated steel, goodbye slate and rubber slate, goodbye clay and concrete tiles.

And keep building with:

Steel cables.

Cross braces.

Anchors.

X-braces

The Accu-Keder system (truss cover attachment).

Light-diffusing fabric—the heaviest: polyethylene multi-layer construction—welded.

High side walls.

Ridge poles.

Cable braces.

Threshold rods.

Construction of the new indoor tennis facility—first called Magnuson Tennis Center and now called TCSP—began in July of 2012. There were delays. There were jitters. As the building grew, so did interest from the tennis community. A place to play and keep playing when the rains came falling.

The building was ready in September 2013.

Made ready for Lester's re-entry and mixed doubles with Player Q.

MIXED DOUBLES MIXUP WITH PLAYER Q

At the end of the next ball machine class, Lester risked saying hello to Player Q—how are you doing? What do you think of the class? How long have you played this fascinating game?

And Player Q replied—hey, bud, you wanta help me out with a game of mixed doubles?

Mixed doubles? Who with?

Couple of ladies, said Player Q.

From the class?

Yeah. Player FA and Player LZ.

Which ones were they? How did you get to know them so fast?

The skinny ones, said Player Q.

He grinned. He winked.

Cherubic.

Lester had to admit it.

He was old.

He was slow on the uptake.

He had not focused on the ladies in the Ball Machine class because he'd been busy worrying about his strokes, his footwork, his attention-span, his eye refusing to watch the ball but looking instead at the net—and at Florian—who looked at Lester like he was a corpse wearing running shoes.

Lester had also continued his bad lifelong habit of looking into the near-future hoping to see what happened after his strings caressed the ball, locking his gaze on the imagined picture-perfect trajectory of the ball in the near-future instead of locking both eyeballs onto the ball itself before the hit.

The seams or the shape, or the shadow, or the clock-face—all those tricks suggested by the smiling pros on You Tube.

Haunted by Florian and Dorian, Lester hadn't paid attention to the women in Ball Machine, but this guy Player Q, another old guy, had recruited two of those unnoticed women to play mixed doubles.

In the ways of the world, Lester lagged way behind Player Q.

Lester hesitated. He almost said no. But he did need to play. He hadn't played yet. He didn't know anyone yet. So he said okay to Player Q—each person in the foursome would pay for a fourth of the court—the fees handled by the ever-efficient Front Desk, and that afternoon, even though his knee throbbed from the light exercise in Ball Machine, Lester found himself joining Player Q on Court 1—the early morning site of their Ball Machine class.

The women were friends. Player FA and Player LZ. Thin edgy frisky women with short hair—adult females who moved like teen-agers. Player Q took Player FA, leaving Lester with Player LZ.

Warming up, Lester saw flaws in the stroke production of Player Q. And when the match started, he saw massive problems in the strokes of his partner.

She hit too hard.

Her ball went out.

Her ball hit the net.

Her ball hit the back-cloth tarp hanging on the wall.

Her ball flew off the court.

And then he noticed that Player Q was telling his partner —Player FA—where to stand. Which grip to use. How to swing.

Player LZ stood close, and Player FA kept nodding, okay-okay, obedient student to ardent teacher.

And Player Q, a muscular guy in his very early 70's, was coming on to her, halfway between a cuddle-up instructor and a task-master.

When the lecture-lesson ended, Player FA marched to the net, one foot in the alley, opening a giant swathe of back-court, ripe for Lester's lob.

So that's what Lester did.

On his first return, Lester lobbed over Player FA's head, forcing Player Q to hustle.

He got there. He didn't have classic strokes, but he was an athlete, solid body, murderous killer instinct, so when he powered the lob back, the ball leaped off his strings, zoomed past Player LZ at the net, leaving no time for Lester to cover the shot.

Point to the enemy. 15-love.

And across the net there was Player Q, standing close to Player FA, gripping her skinny arm, patting her back, whispering in her ear.

Play continued. And while Player Q was getting his kicks snuggling up to these thin young women, Lester was using his time on the court to practice his forehand, trying to hit a good solid Inside-Out slice, driving the ball at an angle into the ad court—the single best shot he had hit so far under the white white ceiling of Magnuson TC.

His slice forehand was hard to return.

His slice backhand was unique—the enemy players reacted like they had never seen a slice before. Lester's lefty serve, a slice that arced to his right as it crossed the net, pulled the receiver wide, opening up a target.

Lester's finesse—when it worked—matched the brute power of Player Q.

❋ ❋ ❋

At 4-3, with Lester and his partner ahead, Player Q took Player FA's arm, whispered in her ear, and pointed his finger at the ceiling.

He was ordering her to lob.

Lester turned to his partner—Watch for the lob, he said.

Player FA's lob was shallow. She had no control.

When she tried to lob over Lester, he pivoted. He watched the ball—a yellow orb turning against the high white ceiling. Bingo.

He nailed three out of four lobs, killed them with his overhead slice, so Player Q directed Player FA to lob over Lester's partner, Player LZ, who scampered to the back court, her face flushed with the joy of competition.

Player LZ reached the lob. But her return was wild, bringing a grin from Player Q. They kept lobbing Lester's partner. She dashed around the court, frantic footfalls, swatting at the ball.

On the sixth lob, Lester called out MINE!

He tracked the flight of the ball. He hated backing up, afraid he would fall, but this one was his.

But Player LZ was new to tennis.

She hadn't played long enough to know the basics.

Her face was red with dashing around the court.

Just as Lester started his swing, he heard footsteps. Out of the corner of his eye, he saw Player LZ, running full tilt, her eyes out of focus, a wild deer crossing a highway—blinded by the headlights—and then Player LZ slammed into Lester.

Oh, Jesus.

He fell, remembering from his other falls to turn so he landed on his hip, and not on his trick knee.

He knew he had landed when he heard the thump of flesh and bone on a hard unforgiving surface. When his shoulder touched down, Lester felt pain. He was worried about his elbow —all those summers when he wore an elbow brace—and when he looked across the net, Player Q was grinning at him.

Player LZ helped Lester to his feet.

Her face was flushed, filled with excitement.

Her eyes sent Lester a message—he was too old for the game of tennis.

She apologized.

Lester told her it was okay.

He walked to the bench for his tennis bag.

Player Q cried out—Where are you going?

Home, Lester said.

Don't tell me you're hurt, guy.

Sorry, Lester said.

The court is reserved, guy. Everyone here paid. We've got 32 minutes on the clock.

See you in Ball machine, Lester said.

But this is doubles! Cried Player Q. You're taking away our fourth!

Lester shook his head. He needed to check his body for cuts and bruises. He said goodbye to Player LZ. She handed him her business card. When she wasn't slamming into her partner on the hard acrylic tennis court, Player LZ was a commercial artist.

As Lester left the court, Player Q called out: Let's do it again, Bud.

Suppressing the jagged-edged memory of Mad Mixed Doubles, Lester needed to find a different path.

A different doorway to Senior Tennis.

A LESSON FROM COACH MB

On his way out of the club, Lester stopped at the Front Desk. He needed advice—where lurks the Hallowed Pathway Back?

He inquired about classes for Seniors. The Front Desk people chatted with him. How long had he been a member? What was his rating? Did he play doubles or singles?

The Front Desk people were friendly, interested, helpful. They put Lester on a waiting list for Senior Drill and Play (SD&P), taught by Coach MB, a great guy, very popular. There were six players in the class, but openings appeared when a player dropped out. Lester was curious about this guy, Coach MB —a popular great guy—so he signed up for a private lesson. The lesson was tomorrow, at five in the afternoon.

Next Day, Five PM, Court 5 at the Magnuson Tennis Center.

Coach MB was friendly and solid-looking. Great handshake, welcoming smile. Lester guessed his age at mid-forties. Oh, nostalgia. The lesson with Coach MB started out with a question: what stroke would Lester like to work on? Lester's brain froze. Everything in his game needed work. Private lessons were pricey. Lester was a penny-pincher. He wanted good value for his money.

He talked about just coming back after a layoff. So he was

happy when the Coach rescued his indecision with an auto mechanic's metaphor—how about a tune-up?

They warmed up. With his rickety knees, Lester had trouble getting to the ball. He felt like a klutz. He felt like he had sunk to a 1.5 rating. Across the net, Coach MB understood right away, and placed the ball where it was easier to hit. Lester was huffing, he felt ragged. Like he was just learning the game. The Coach chatted about tactics—if you need more time, then you need to hit what kind of shot?

High and deep, Lester said.

Very good. So when you hit your forehand, drive it high and deep to my backhand corner.

So Lester did that. He hit high and deep. He felt the ball on his strings. He felt his control coming back. When the ball went where he wanted, Lester felt better. Maybe he could still play tennis, after all.

❋ ❋ ❋

Fifteen minutes into the lesson, Coach MB asked to see Lester's racket, his vintage Prince. He did not make a smart remark about ancient equipment, but he handed Lester a Wilson and said Try this. They started hitting again. The Wilson felt like a dream-stick. It was lighter than his Prince. It had better balance. When Lester made contact with the ball, his arm did not vibrate. He was thinking he needed a new racket. He was wondering about the price. How much was a dream-stick like this?

Lester had grown up in a household where nothing was wasted. Nothing tossed that could be used. As a kid growing up in Texas, he had collected empty soft-drink bottles—Coke and Dr. Pepper—and redeemed them at the local grocery store for 2 cents apiece.

Lester was about to turn 80.

To join the new tennis world, he needed a new racket.

But he was still tight with his money.

They finished up by hitting volleys. Coach MB said the backhand volley was Lester's best shot. Lester was so hungry for praise that he didn't tell Coach MB about the Rod Laver photo on the cover of Tennis magazine, the photo that showed Laver down on one knee, his body down below the level of the net, hitting a volley, his head turned toward the string-bed, his eye glued to the contact point—ball on strings—that same day Laver won the Grand Slam using his Dunlop Maxply.

When the lesson was done, Lester and the Coach shook hands. Lester felt hope returning. Lester wanted to talk about tennis. About his game, about Senior Drill and Play—but the next lesson was here, a smiling woman in a pricey tennis outfit, her Wealthy Wife smile revealing a set of gleaming picture-perfect teeth.

From the railing of the mezzanine, Lester watched Coach MB's lesson. The woman had great strokes, a solid, enviable Modern forehand, complete with the wrap-around follow-through, a solid two-handed backhand that made a pop when she hit the ball, which she always got to, which meant she was decades younger than Lester. But this woman, a stranger, spurred Lester to get with it. Someday, if he worked hard, his shots might be half as smooth.

❊ ❊ ❊

When Lester got home, his wife said there was a phone call from the tennis club. Lester called the Front Desk. A slot had opened up in SD&P. Lester could join the group. Lester was excited—more contact with Coach MB.

As he finished registering for SD&P—his fee discounted for missing the first three weeks—Lester felt like a knight-quester on the trail of the Holy Grail—a twilight arrival at the gateway to a mysterious castle (Chapel Perilous), where he would be met by a guide, the same way Virgil the Poet guided Dante the poet into the labyrinth, the archetypal storyline—descent into the underworld—in the Divine Comedy.

Was Lester's guide Coach MB?

Or was it one of the helpful people-helpers who manned the Front Desk?

THE FINE ART OF SOCIAL EXCLUSION

On his way out of the club, Lester stopped at the Front Desk to inquire about Complimentary Senior Doubles. A pleasant woman charted the routine:

Play was from 8:15 to 9:25, five days a week.

Seniors 65 or older got 70-75 minutes of play on two courts at no charge.

Players onsite decided how to pair-up.

Sign-ups were Saturday morning, at 9 AM.

And again on Sunday morning, if you wanted more play.

Lester put his name on the waiting list for Friday. He wasn't expecting a call, but it came on Thursday afternoon, from the Front Desk.

Lester felt a thrill—he was going to play real doubles. Then he felt a chill. What if he wasn't hitting that day? What if he was the oldest senior? What if he was the slowest? Was he going to allow his age to be a problem? He carried this worrisome weight to his car. He carried it in the passenger seat as he headed west toward home. He gave himself a pep talk.

He was alive. He could still move. He was re-learning the game from a world-class coach. So what if he might hit a few crappy shots? So what if he disappointed his partner? Lester needed tennis. Tennis was his life-blood.

* * *

Lester arrived at the club at 7:46. Play would start in 29 minutes. He used the bathroom. He loved the senior stall. He went through his Health Club warm-up, pendulum leg swings to loosen the hip-bones—back and forth, medium swings until he warmed up, then long swings, right leg, left leg—balancing himself by holding onto a high table in the mezzanine.

He followed the pendulums with circular leg swings, 30 to the right, 30 to the left—both legs.

He followed the leg swings with arm-swings, rotating the arms in unison and then staccato—left-right, left-right—feeling his shoulders warm up. He bounced the ball on the racket strings 50 times without missing, making sure his eyes stuck to the ball.

At 8:10, from the mezzanine, Lester watched two senior players take over Court 6. They knew each other. They warmed up, soft shots in the service box. To Lester's eye, they looked smooth, confident, youngish, exclusive. Lester's nerves rattled—if he ever got on a court with them, how would he do against these guys?

Lester made his way to the courts, observing the foursome on Court 6, four excellent players, hitting now from the back court, showing quality strokes. No one paid any attention to Lester. No nods, no hellos.

As he set down his backpack on Court 5, he saw movement behind the green flap doorway at the back wall. Two women emerged. Women younger than Lester, dressed in pricey-looking track suits, one canary yellow, one chartreuse. Lester introduced himself. Feeling over-generous, but edgy because he was the new guy, Lester popped a can of new balls.

Hi, he said. I'm Lester.

The Chartreuse track suit was Player GC.

The Canary Yellow was Player JL.

The women warmed up on the same side, hitting against

Lester, side-to-side, making him hustle, as if they were teaming up—the women vs. the men. Player GC had good ball control. Player JL did not. Trying to be polite, Lester kept his shots soft, remembering not to hit with lots of spin. When he hit three frame shots in a row, the women gave each other a look. What was this old dude doing here, anyway?

※ ※ ※

The back wall curtain parted and here came the fourth, a round-faced man with a perpetual preacher's smile, a full head of white hair, and a pricey baby-blue tennis suit. The women warbled their hellos.

Lester shook hands. The smiling man was Player OR. He had a soft pudgy handshake. He hustled around the court like a chubby rabbit. His shots were okay. Lester was trying to focus, but Player JL had started to hit harder, forcing Lester to block the ball back with a tiny bit of spin for control, which brought a dirty look from across the net when his dink-ball return touched down and then shot sideways.

The reigning threesome decided it would be fun to play girls against the boys. The women served first, using the pancake grip, push-popping slow balls into the service court. Lester's partner, showing off for the girls, slapped the first return into the back wall. On the next serve, when the softie came to Lester, he returned the ball with side-spin, forcing the server, approaching the net, to lunge when she saw his ball jerking sideways. She caught the ball on the racket frame, slapping it sideways into the mesh curtain that divided Courts 5 and 6.

She glared at Lester, eyes bright with anger.

What's your name again?

Lester.

You're new here, right?

Couple of weeks.

I hate your slice, she said. It's really nasty.

* * *

With his partner missing her shots and Lester's spin-balls zig-zagging, the score held steady until Lester tried to finish it in the grand manner, treating his foursome to the unorthodox remembered power of his squat-overhead smash, a shot he had used twenty years ago—when he could still move.

Squatting down hurt.

Lester felt off-balance.

He locked his eyes onto the ball.

He swung the racket, the hammer grip.

He felt the strings grab the ball.

The trajectory felt like old times. But then the ball landed. It missed the back line by two feet.

Lester felt bad.

He had wanted to show off. Make an impression, make his mark.

Lester's out-ball ended the set. Without consulting the men, the two women put their heads together. Without consulting Lester or his partner, Player GC joined Lester. She took the ad-court.

Player GC walked to the baseline.

From this side of the net, with Player GC as his partner, Lester saw what she was doing with her serve. It was soft and high, a blimpy ball, but it always hit the court—and it gave the returner trouble, forcing errors on the return, and now Lester was re-thinking Senior Doubles—maybe there was another way to play this game when you got old.

Maybe a 79-year-old man without much athletic ability did not have to follow in the professional footsteps of Rosewall and Arthur Ashe and this new hot-shot, Roger Federer.

Maybe there was room for Lester on the magical courts at Magnuson.

And then he remembered that his new partner, Player GC,

had not missed a single serve in the first set. And then her ball sailed past Lester, good net clearance, dropping down an inch in front of the service line, and making trouble for chubby Player OR, who hit the ball at Lester, who put away a zinger of a volley.

Lester spoke to Player GC —Good serve, partner.

Player GC nodded. She nailed three more serves, three blooper returns that extracted errors from the enemy, and then Player JL was serving and Lester was feeling sharper now, his ancient Prince racket transformed into a sword, Excalibur III, and Lester's accurate slices drove the opposition wild, and with the steady, smart play of his partner, Lester's team took the set 6-0.

Player GC said:

Changed my mind—I love that slice of yours.

A buzzer buzzed. The clock read 9:27. Senior doubles was over. Across the mesh screen-divider, two of the players on Court 6 were looking at Lester. One of them gave him a thumbs-up.

The other one said: You ever hit a flat ball?

I keep trying, Lester said.

*　*　*

No one invited Lester for coffee. And when he climbed the stairs to the mezzanine, he saw his three court-mates standing in line at Willy's Café. Their backs were turned. They were chatting like old friends. They had forgotten Lester.

He could have been angry.

He could have been hurt.

He could have crashed the magic circle.

He told himself that his goal was not learning the dance steps of senior social tennis.

His goal was staying alive.

He turned around, walked back down the stairs.

His knees hurt—a senior player bio-alert, a call for the ice-pack.

He was worried about his knees.

SD&P WITH COACH MB

As a college teacher, Lester had been successful because of a simple technique: On the first day of class, the teacher's job is clear:

Find out who's in the room.

To earn his PhD, Lester had spent 9 years in college. Four years for the B.A., two years for his M.A., and three years for his PhD. Sitting in the classrooms as a student, Lester had studied the techniques of multiple scholars trying to be teachers. What worked and what didn't.

Most professors opened by talking about themselves. Their degrees, their publications, their academic awards. A few were funny. The worst teachers splattered the walls with their egos.

The better professors opened by charting the course—where this hard-earned sacred knowledge held inside the professor's head would take the students sitting mute in their hard seats for a whole semester. The great lecturers showed off. The dullards made bad jokes.

So when he got his first T.A. job (Teaching Assistant is a lower serf-class PhD candidate teaching on the side to make enough money to stay in school long enough to finish the PhD work), Lester started his first class not with a lecture, not with a brief history of the novel in Europe and America, but with a five-minute writing on their last year in high school: It was early September. Three months ago, the students in his class had been seniors graduating high school.

Lester printed out the topic on the white-board.

"This weirdo thing that happened to me during my last year in high school English class."

They wrote for five minutes.

Then they read aloud.

The girls wrote better than the guys.

A girl from Eagle Pass wrote about loving Jane Eyre. She was here on campus to meet her own Mr. Rochester

A guy from Dallas wrote about fighting over a girl in a parking lot in San Antonio's Bun 'n' Barrel Drive-in. His reading got a thumbs-up from the guys. As people read their words, the class changed from a motley group of strangers into a cadre of seekers eager to share their adventures.

❆ ❆ ❆

And that's what Coach MB had done in Lester's tennis lesson—finding out where Lester was coming from in his tennis game, where he wanted to go—dreams, aspirations, survival, weaknesses—and the same generous curiosity showed up in Senior Drill and Play on a chilly Tuesday in November, where five senior tennis players were warming up hitting slow-balls, a controlled short-court warm-up that forced the players to hit with control.

The Coach waved at Lester to take his place across from a tall woman, blonde, with a smooth forehand that came from taking lessons as a child. All those people who'd had early lessons exuded confidence hitting groundstrokes.

Not Lester. He was nervous. He was late joining the class—they had been learning for three weeks—so today was his audition. Lester warned himself to be nice. No professorial smart remarks. These people were not his students. They were his tennis colleagues.

Six players on the court, four in the alleys, two hitting down the T. The players hit soft shots while Coach MB observed, offered suggestions. Only 15 minutes in and Lester was happy about the class. He felt right at home. This was the short-court technique used by Dennis Van Der Meer in that weeklong tennis seminar in Redlands, California—how long ago was that? — where Van Der Meer had nailed Lester by classifying him (whispering to his blonde assistant, who wrote on her clipboard) as a decent B club player.

Each time the players rotated, changing hitting partners, Lester was careful to introduce himself—Hi, I'm Lester, Player LE —and to note the names of his fellow-students. Two guys, Players PH and JS. Three women, Player JD, Player GS, and Player NA.

Player JD was tiny and quick, with great reflexes and a deceptive lob. Player NA moved fast and hit everything hard. Player GS was tall, with a killer forehand—and (Lester found out later) married to Player JS.

Player PH was solid, with ripply white hair, a natural forehand topspin, a lightning-fast sense of humor, and eyebrows that needed trimming. Player JS, the other guy, was tall—maybe 6-3—with eyes that showed intelligence, and strokes that had come from that sacred unattainable back-story sanctum, early childhood coaching.

❋ ❋ ❋

Maybe by chance, maybe by pre-ordination, Lester had landed in the perfect tennis class. Six players in SD&P—three women, two guys, and Lester the oldest, Lester the crippled newbie. The smooth movements of his classmates bespoke youth on the court—good for Lester, tough on the others.

All five of his drill-mates hit good clean balls. Every player had a solid forehand. Everyone could move better than Lester with his bad knees. They seemed younger and, as Lester found out, they were younger. At 79, Lester was the oldest member of the class, with a lot to prove. He was three weeks late starting. Another senior had dropped out. He was taking her spot.

Without the game-pressure of winning and scoring, Lester could focus on hitting the ball, on improving his ragged shots left over from the sixties, the wood rackets, the Don Budge follow-through.

After the warm-up the players stood in two lines while Coach MB fed the ball. The players in the deuce court hit forehands. The players in the ad-court hit backhands. The goal was to place each shot close to the singles alley. Bad backhands showed up fast.

Lester missed three slice backhands in a row. His slice forehand ball kept hitting the tape. Coach MB changed Lester's forehand grip to a modified Eastern. In the ready position, the racket face closes, looking downward. In the Continental, the racket face opens up—easier on the slice.

The change was miraculous. Lester's topspin shots were now more solid. There was a pop when the strings met the ball. With that resounding pop, Lester felt a surge of hope—maybe he had a future in senior tennis after all.

* * *

After the drills, they played Deadly Doubles—starting at 15-30, putting the service team two points away from losing the game. The 15-30 put pressure on the first server. Miss a shot that loses the game and you rotated out. Sitting on the sidelines, waiting for someone to miss the ball, Lester felt lucky. He had made it through his first class. These were nice people. Had he found the tennis friends he'd been looking for?

When it was Lester's turn, his stomach fluttered. Here came the nerves. He double-faulted his first serve. The score was now 15-40. He got the next serve in, felt his slice spin-ball coming back. At 30-40, he saw Player NA shifting to her left—so she could take his lefty spin-ball on her forehand. So instead of giving her that shot, Lester aimed for the backhand corner, forcing her to reach for a backhand. He got lucky. The ball skidded, pushing Player NA to her left. She fluffed a backhand service return, hitting a soft squishy ball right into the racket of Player PH, who put the ball away. With vigor.

The score went to deuce. Fired by his instant success, Lester lost his perspective and his serve—had his edginess caused him to hit a bad shot? He double-faulted, ad-out. And then Player JD, with her backhand, killed Lester's shot.

❊ ❊ ❊

Sitting on the sidelines, watching his new friends playing senior doubles, Lester analyzed his situation. The class was too short—75 minutes was not enough, and Lester needed more instruction, more tips to guide him into this new world called Senior Tennis.

He had wasted years by not playing—and now he had too much to re-learn. The 15-30 game with its lop-sided scoring squeezed him, made him think. Made it hard to breathe. After what he had learned today, his world opened wide—too much to learn before he was dead.

But this SD&P class—the drills, the focus, the pressure of serving
the first ball at 15-30—was just what he needed. Lester shook his head. He was in the iron grip of fatigue. He needed to get in shape. He needed to work on his serve.

A buzzer rang. His first 75 minutes of Senior Drill and Play was over. Coach MB gathered the class at the net-post. He asked what they had learned. No one spoke. That was Lester's opening.

Eastern forehand grip, Lester said.

Instead of what? the Coach said.

Instead of the Continental.

Anyone else? the Coach said.
Show us how to return Lester's serve, said Player NA .
Can do, the Coach said. Have a good week.

* * *

Lester walked out with Player PH.
He said: You have a wicked sense of humor.
Player PH said: And you have a wicked slice.
Lester: If I had your forehand, I wouldn't need a slice.
Player PH: See you next week.
Lester: How do you like your Head racket?
Player PH: Does the job.
Lester: Maybe I can hit with it sometime—try it out for feel.
Player PH: Absolutely.

* * *

That first day in Senior Drill and Play Lester had a feeling of finding the Grail. Half a dozen solid senior players, everyone was smart, well-educated, polite. Six old people moving like pros on this journey together, trying to get better at tennis, what a beautiful game. With help from this group, Lester could keep going. At 79, his old arthritic bones had a tennis future at last.

And he had found his guide to the labyrinths of Senior Tennis.

The affable Coach MB.

LESTER MAKES A TENNIS FRIEND

Lester was on the mezzanine at TCSP, doing his warm-up routine before SD&P, when Player PH arrived. Lester said hello. Player PH said hello back. He eyed Lester's warm-up routine. He did not join in. He did not ask what Lester was doing. Instead, he asked if Lester would like to hit practice balls sometime.

    Sure, Lester said.
    Where? said Player PH.
    I've got a court. Half a block from my house.
    When? said Player PH.
    How about Monday?

They settled on a time. Lester checked Dark Sky, his friendly weather app. Monday looked okay. It rained on Saturday. On Sunday, the Big Fog shrouded the neighborhood. On Monday, knowing there would be puddles on the courts, Lester brought a push-broom. He was pushing water, spreading the puddles out, when Player PH arrived, waving from the top of the stairs.

Lester's new tennis friend moved well on the court. No waste motion and his forehand was perfect and effortless. With a very short backswing, and a lightning fast forward motion, Player PH could hit winners off Lester's serve, most of them cross-court.

The workout made Lester happy. Player PH wanted practice in returning serves. Lester wanted practice in following his serve to the net, getting set-up for the volley. His knees would never get that far, but he was happy if he made it to the service line.

Player PH was strong. His upper body was solid, which made for an efficient swing. When he connected with a forehand, Player PH's torso rotated, easy, automatic, without any fuss. The official tennis term for the rotation is Unit Turn. The unit is your upper body, your hips, and your hitting arm. When Lester watched professionals playing on TV, instead of tracking the ball, he kept his eye on the closest player—noting the set-up, the free hand pointing at the oncoming ball, the Unit Turn, the moment of contact.

It was great to have a tennis friend.

And Lester envied the automatic unit turn.

And he tried to analyze, yet again, why his unit turn was not automatic.

Maybe it was because he had started out with a wood racket.

ON THE COURT WITH COACH MB

Coach MB starts every SD&P class with a short-court warm-up—all six players just behind the service line, four hitters hitting down the alleys (2 and 2), two hitting along the center service line. About three minutes in, Coach MB stops the warm-ups. He does a demo to remind the group: Remember your footwork during the warm-up.

Don't just stand there looking all tall and pretty, he says. Get your body into the ready position. Racquet in both hands. Lower your center of gravity. Then drive up from your legs into the ball.

It's all feet and legs, the Coach says. Let your feet do more work. After you hit the ball, get right back into the ready position.

The warmup drill today shifts the action to all six players at the net, keeping the ball low. And inside the service courts, hitting cross-court.

Players A and B hit from alley to alley. Their ball crosses close to the middle of the net, marked by the net strap.

Players C and D hit from one deuce court to the other.

Players E and F hit from one ad court to the other.

It's very crowded.

If the players lurch, they run into another player.

If they hit too hard, the rally stops.

After 3 minutes, the Coach calls Rotate.

Lester likes this drill because it calls for a lot of slice. When he's in the alley, hitting along the net-tape, he feels extra-special—he reminds himself that he's leading a charmed life. Several friends have died. Other friends are sick. He feels lucky. He feels blessed.

❋ ❋ ❋

The lesson today is the topspin forehand and the backhand slice. The players form two lines. The Coach feeds three balls. The players hit heavy forehands. Everyone but Lester uses the eastern forehand grip. Lester has to remind himself to switch grips—Continental to eastern, Continental to eastern. When the players have some success, the Coach pauses for a demo:
Eastern grip.
Both hands on the racket.
Shoulder rotation on the backswing.
Double-checking the racket face—it should look down at the court.
Footwork on the hit.
Follow-through with the windshield washer motion.
Now the Coach drops little flat markers to create targets.
Everyone starts missing.
The players slow down.
They focus on hitting the targets.
After ten minutes, they pick up balls. Lester hurries to grab a wire pickup basket—he's having right knee troubles. It's painful for him to squat. When he leans down for a ball, his back squawks.
For the slice backhand, the Coach shifts everyone to the Continental. Lester shivers with joy. He feels smug. He's been using the Continental grip for decades. It's his signature shot. Hitting a solid slice backhand makes him feel like a gunslinger. The Coach uses Lester to demonstrate the stroke.
Lester misses three out of five.

The Coach pauses. Lester takes a deep breath. The next demo-shots are better. Lester is a silly old man. Give him a twitch of limelight and his ego goes berserk. He reminds himself: tennis is a game, buddy. We play games to relax. We play tennis to be precise. Lester plays tennis because he loves aiming the ball. Lester's lecture to himself lasts through the backhand drills, but it slinks away when the players pair off for doubles—the "play" portion of SD&P.

※ ※ ※

Lester pairs up with Player JD.

She likes the deuce court.

Because of his lefty slice backhand, Lester also likes the deuce court. When the serve comes, Player JD lofts a lob over the head of the net person, who's standing too close to the net.

First point to the good guys,

Love-fifteen. Lester focuses on his return using bounce-hit.

Across the net, the enemy bounces the ball three times.

Bounce.

Bounce.

Bounce.

Hit.

Bounce on Lester's side. He whispers hit as his strings make contact for a backhand slice.

Lester gets lucky.

The ball feels good on his strings.

The feel good emotion zaps his brain.

His brain shoots the good feeling to his heart.

Lester's ball, loaded with slice from the lesson, curves away from his strings, arcs itself across the net, keeps spinning as it touches down in the enemy alley.

Spin! cries Enemy 1.

I got it! cries Enemy 2.

The ball floats back, puffy, slow, like a fistful of feathers.

Player JD, a fearless net rusher, kills the fluffball at the net. She touches her racket to Lester's racket.

The smile on her face. The gleam in her eyes. That's why Lester loves this game. Seven minutes later, Coach MB calls Time! Let's pick up! Following the ball pickups, the players form a circle while Coach MB asks what they learned today—and when he comes around to Lester —there is a pause.

Lester grins.

Eastern Forehand grip, he says, on the Modern Forehand.

See you next week, says the Coach.

The stalwart members of SD&P grab coats, sweaters, racket bags, purses. They form a line going up the stairs to Willy's Café. While they order at the window. Lester and Player PH pull two tables together.

Six chairs.

Six coffees. Six senior players, all still alive. This is Lester's Group. His Tennis Gang. The talk flows from topic to topic. Lester nods.

All because of this tennis class. All because of Coach MB, his tennis brain, his sense of humor, and that magnificent Nike Swoosh forehand.

THE MAN WITH THE NIKE SWOOSH FOREHAND

You pull open the front door to the TCSP. The cold wind pushes you inside. Warm in here. Back home again.
    You say hello to the Front Desk helpers. You say hello to Player DC, stringing a racket in the Pro shop. And then, from Court 2, you hear the voice of Coach MB.
    A big voice calling LET'S GO.
    A big playground voice urging the players on.
    His voice carries you up the stairs to Willy's Café.
    Let's Goooo!
    You say Buenos Dias to Willy.
    He chuckles hearing your accent.
    You order an Americano.
    You watch from the mezzanine.
    Coach MB down there on Court 2 with a roller basket full of yellow tennis balls.
    He stands between the baseline and the green back curtain.
    He's feeding balls with his Swoosh Forehand.
    Ball to the ad court.
    Again. Again. Again.
    Across the net from the Swoosh Forehand—four women 3.5

players—four women running.

They pause to hit the ball.

They run to their next location.

On the Coach's side of the net, four more women.

Eight women players on the court, running and getting set and hitting.

Feet flashing as they run.

Loving their time on the court with Coach MB:

A compact, athletic man instructing eight women players on a single court in a drill where the first hitter returns from the deuce-court baseline, then from the sixty-foot line, then from the Queen Spot (two feet in front of the service line, three feet from the center line)—while her partner returns from the ad-court baseline.

If a hitter mis-hits, Coach MB feeds two more balls.

Forcing the other players to hang loose.

Two tries and two misses and Coach MB waves the player along—make room for the next hitter.

* * *

Coach MB teaches 35 classes a week at TCSP.

One of those is Boot Camp. Sixteen players on 4 courts, starting at 5:30 AM on Tuesdays and Thursdays.

The tennis part of Boot Camp is playing tie-breaks—the winner gets to seven games first.

If you win a tie-break, you move toward the wall.

If you lose, you move in the opposite direction, toward the door.

The oldest veteran of Boot-Camp quit after nine faithful years when he turned 74—he kept getting closer and closer to the door and saw the handwriting in small black letters on the door handle.

Senior Player, Exit Here.

In between playing the tie-breaks and scoring, the Boot

Campers do exercises to stay in shape: alternating push-ups with burpees (Squat, Plank, Push-Up, Back to Squat, Jump up from the Squat Position) racing lines, doing fitness circuits.

Coach MB likes to stay in shape—so he makes sure to do his Burpees.

Coach MB is 53.

His height is 5-9.

His build is solid and fluidly athletic.

He can still run fast.

His Swoosh Forehand is a wondrous thing to behold. Enviable. Sturdy. Magical.

The forehand of today sprouted from a sawed-off Jack Kramer Autograph, made of wood, painted green, fashioned by his dad, the head tennis coach at The University of Oregon in Eugene, when Coach MB was three years old, gripping the sawed-off Jack Kramer, tracing the swing-path of the forehand, following the fluid lines of a Nike Swoosh trade-mark.

The Nike Swoosh symbol was painted on a sheet of plywood attached to another sheet, forming a secure hitting corner for the three-year old Coach MB, which produced the fluid motion, the essence of control, which creates maximum confidence on the tennis courts at TCSP—some half-century later.

In addition to Boot Camp, Coach MB teaches 34 other classes at TCSP.

Three of these classes are SD&P (the acronym for Senior Drill and Play).

Tuesday AM at 8:15 (3.0).

Wednesday AM at 8:15 (3.0).

Thursday AM at 8:15 (2.5).

❈ ❈ ❈

Because Coach MB generates so much fun on the court, an observer might think that this guy has been teaching tennis all his life. It's a fact that he inherited the tennis gene from his dad.

It's also a fact that he had the all-important early training, and that he played tennis in high school, but in college Coach MB switched from tennis to varsity water-polo, and his team played well enough to join the Goodwill Games, where they competed against swimmers like Matt Biondi, an Olympic gold medalist.

In college, Coach MB managed music stores for Wherehouse Entertainment and Tower Records, which put him in touch with young energetic musicians, players in bands that hit the road, traveling minstrels bringing music to the multitudes. The band his company produced was called Candlebox, and they had signed a lucrative contract with Madonna's Maverick Co., and then here came the lawyers from Warner Brothers, and there went the money.

* * *

Meanwhile, Coach MB and his wife had a baby on the way—but the open road is no place to raise a child—so he deployed the management skills he had polished in the music business and managing traveling minstrels of the early 1990's by taking a dive into the Food business.

He was the corporate training manager at Wild Ginger and managing Seattle restaurants like Cafe Minnie's, Snoose Junction and Alley Cat, and from that turning to restaurant supply—where he and his wife created 7,000 sandwiches and salads a week for Boeing, Evergreen Hospital, Northwest Hospital, Tacoma General, Harborview—plus 20 independent food shops—and all the time Coach MB was polishing the people skills needed to make a fine tennis instructor.

All he needed was to be touched by a tennis angel.

That angel turned out to be his dad.

Coach MB's re-entry into tennis started when he hurt his shoulder playing soccer.

With soccer on the sidelines, Coach MB followed a suggestion from his dad to attend a Wednesday evening at the

Central Park Tennis Club in Kirkland, where a tennis pro named Phil Ansdell ran a program called Phil's Drills.

For nine weeks, Coach MB hung out at Phil's Drills. He had been gone from tennis for two decades—and now he liked being back on the court again.

He felt right at home.

One night Coach MB was helping some players with their shots and Phil Ansdell, liking what he saw, suggested that Coach MB take the USPTA (United States Professional Tennis Association) qualifying exam—which he aced, but he needed some teaching experience, so he asked Lisa M (All-American, played number one at the UW) if he could observe her teaching methods.

In a token payment, he promised to bring coffee. He also promised to steal one of his dad's sleeveless sweaters. Lisa M knew Vern Ball—the man of a thousand sweaters—as "Sweater Guy." She said okay, partner, follow my lead.

Showing a lot of class, Lisa M accepted the stolen sweater; then she gave it back when Coach MB's follow-sessions were over.

※ ※ ※

Melding his new tennis acumen with his hospitality skills—Coach MB applied for a coaching job at TCSP, back in the early days, when it was called Magnuson Tennis Center.

As a tennis coach, he was unknown.

As an unknown coach, he was competing against applications from all over the world—tennis pros wanted to work at Magnuson.

The club turned him down.

Their reason: the club already employed 7 tennis coaches. There was no need for one more.

(How things change: At the time of this writing, TCSP employs 26 coaches.)

But there was a big remodel going on at the club—not just the courts, but also the Mezzanine Café (soon to become Willy's Café)—so Coach MB made management a deal: he would take the job of Café Manager, with the caveat that he could teach half a dozen courses.

His schedule after six months:

Forty hours a week at TCSP.

Forty hours as a food-vendor.

Coach MB was one busy guy.

"If I had an hour between classes," he says. "Then I would climb into the car, race to Cash-and-Carry on Aurora, load up with supplies for salads and sandwiches, and race back to the club in time for my next class."

But that schedule went away when the club gave Coach MB more classes. And three of those were Senior Drill and Play.

One clue to the expertise of Coach MB—he has to maintain his own tennis game, and his own tennis pro brain. Here's Coach MB talking about the rigors of the Elite Professional:

"In order to get an APC rating, you must attend 20 hours of classwork annually for 3 years. You can complete a portion online—with approved seminars. Then there are two tests: Performance to test your strokes, and a written test with 200 questions on history, business, grips, proshop mechanicals.

"For the performance tests, the candidates are fed 10 balls in which you have to hit 9/10 in a specific spot. So 9/10 for each lane of forehands, slice, topspin etc. Serves and drop shots are 5/6 to specific spots. You only get one set of balls per shot per test. If you don't pass your level, you have to wait and be retested at a later date."

TACTICAL TENNIS E-MAILS

When Lester's knees kept him off the court, he asked Player PH to update him about the class. That request unleashed the artful brain of Player PH, himself the proud owner of a Swoosh forehand—quick, natural, deadly.

E-Mail: Player PH to Player LE

Hi, Lester. You missed a great class. Today the Coach ran us through another version of the 4-2. But first, we warmed up—seven minutes:

First, 45 secs – we did slices in the short court. Don't let ball go beyond service line.

Second, 2 minutes: The Coach moved us back to the baseline to hit groundstrokes. Concentrate on the follow-through, he said, and go for maximum spin. Move as little as possible, take your time, and don't rush the warm-up. Let the ball bounce twice if necessary, forces you to go for low balls.

Third, 1 minute: You or the enemy come up for volleys (inside service line). Feeder stays back at baseline. Concentrate on continuing to look at your racket head even AFTER you have hit the volley.

Fourth, 1 minute: Switch who feeds, who volleys.

Fifth, 2 minutes: Serving practice. You should be able to hit at least 15-20 serves, first and second.

Total time: 7 minutes.

When we finished warming up, Coach MB called out the name of the drill, the 4-2.

The Coach rolled his basket of balls to the baseline, between players C and D. His ball, each hit with the forehand, will simulate a serve, starting the point.

Player D in the ad court.

Player C in the deuce court.

Across the net, facing the Coach, are Players A and B—they are the receivers. Player A, in the deuce court, stands at the sixty-foot line. Player B, in the ad court, takes the Queen Spot, two feet in front of the service line, close to the center.

By feeding the ball to Player A's backhand, the Coach forces a return to the enemy's deuce court, to Player C's forehand. For most seniors ranked 2.5 or 3.0, the forehand is their main stroke. With an early shoulder turn, Player A could whip a backhand down the center. With a good knee-bend, Player A could get under the Coach's ball and loft a high lob. But the percentage shot from Player A is still cross-court to the enemy forehand.

Later in this drill, the Coach will do a change-up, feeding the ball to Player A's backhand. Will Player A be ready?

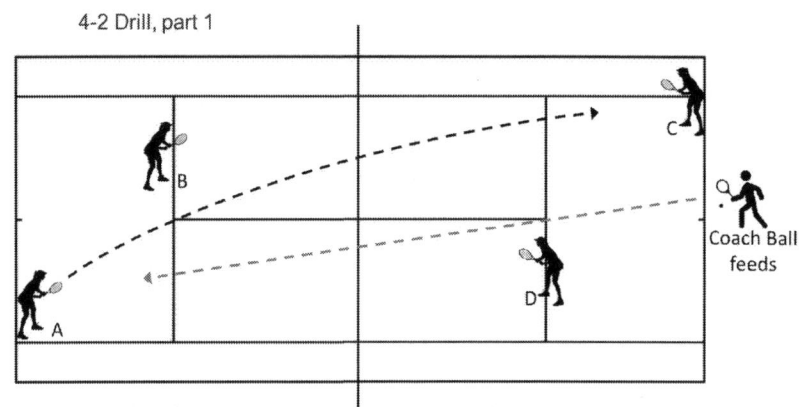

4-2 Drill, part 1

Coach Ball feeds to Player A's backhand in the deuce court.
Player A returns the ball to C. The foursome plays out the point.

Next: Coach MB feeds down the center line to Player B's forehand in the ad court. Player B returns cross-court to Player

D—that's the high percentage shot. To hit the ball to Player C, Player B would need to set up early, knees bent, the ready position—taking up more time. To change the rhythm of play, Players C and D could leave the baseline and move closer to the net.

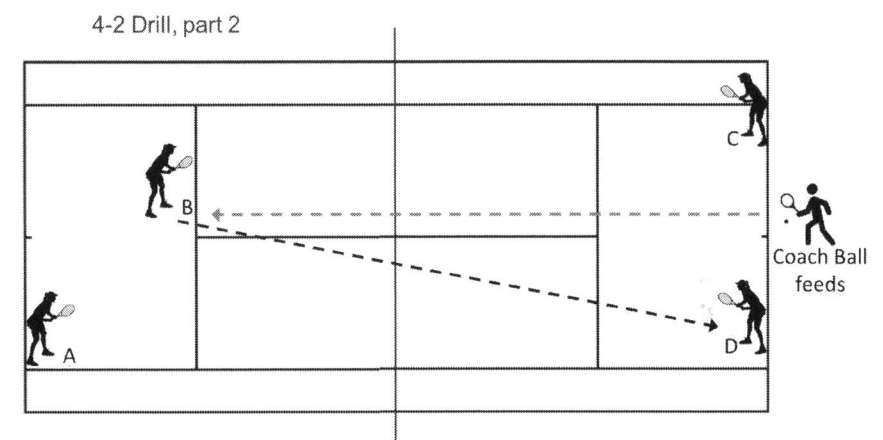

4-2 Drill, part 2

Coach Ball feeds down the center line to Player B's forehand in the ad court. Player B returns cross court to Player D. The foursome plays out the point.

Next: This 4-2 drill helps all four players to change their play: the baseline is the thing you stand behind to serve. After the serve, move up.

Player D has moved up! Coach MB feeds cross-court to Player A's backhand. The foursome plays out the point.

4-2 Drill, part 3

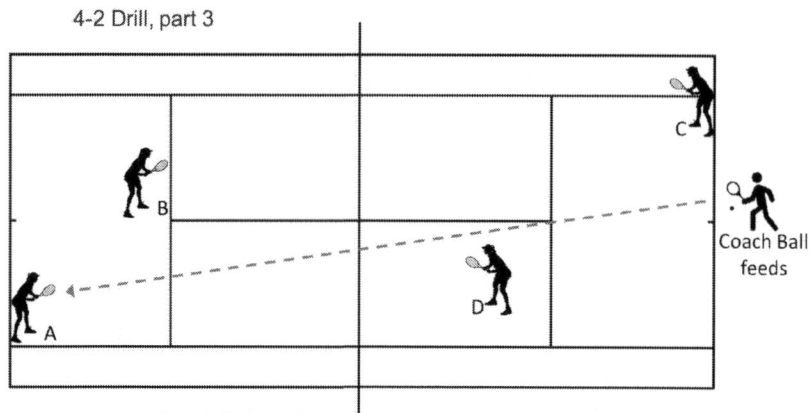

Coach Ball feeds cross court to Player A's backhand.
The foursome plays out the point.

Coach MB feeds a medium-speed forehand ball to Player A.

Player A returns the ball cross-court to Player C.

Player C slams the ball at Player B, who volleys cross-court to Player D's backhand.

The foursome plays out the point.

4-2 Drill, part 4

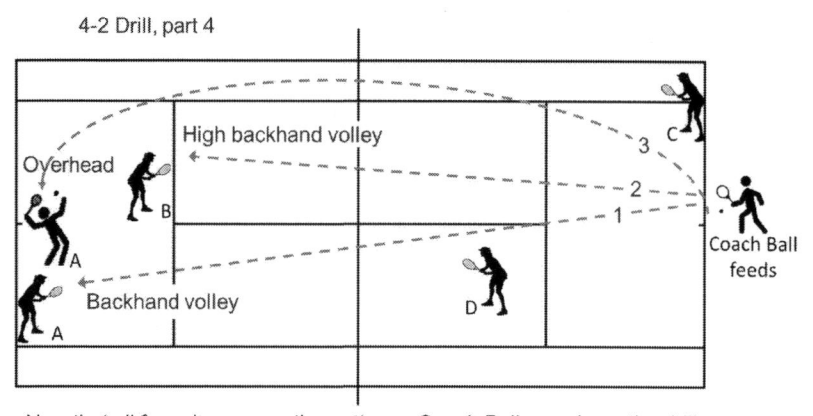

Now that all four players see the patterns, Coach Ball speeds up the drill.
One ball forces Player A to hit a backhand volley.
The next ball forces Player B to hit a high backhand volley.
The last ball to Player A is a lob, forcing Player A to hit an overhead.
 Rotate.

Big theme today from Coach MB was "demeanor," esp.

a positive demeanor. It started with a pep talk about how everyone could choose to be upbeat. Then he focused on tennis. Don't be intimidated. "I own this net, you're not going to take it from me." All very inspirational.

At the end of the drill, when all six Senior Players have gone through the same process, Coach MB asked how long does the average senior foursome take to play a senior doubles point:

Answer: 22 seconds.

We miss you, Lester. Hurry and get well.

PART II

USE YOUR HEAD IN SENIOR TENNIS

BODY-WORK: LESTER WARMS UP

From a coach at a local health club, Lester learned a five-minute warm-up that got his blood moving and relaxed his brain, which he needed if he was going up against a couple of big (younger) hitters in Senior Comp Doubles.

First, Lester finds a wall, a doorway, or a kitchen counter-top 36 inches high.

With his right hand on the counter-top, Lester swings his right leg 30 times, back and forth, loosening the right hip.

Then he makes a 180-turn, left hand on the counter-top, and swings his left leg 30 times.

Bracing himself with both hands on the counter-top, Lester circles the right leg 30 times clockwise. Then 30 times counter-clockwise.

He repeats that circular motion with the left leg.

Squatting in the Ready Position, Lester swings both arms in a clockwise motion, loosening the shoulders.

Still squatting, he swings both arms in a counter-clockwise circle.

With the blood coursing through him, Lester feels warmer.

Taking the racket in his left hand, he bounces the tennis ball off the strings, counting to 50.

He repeats the bouncing ball for the right hand.

And fluffs only two.

If he's at home in his basement, Lester ricochets a tennis ball off the front door of his vintage basement fridge. He tosses with his left hand, he tries to predict the bounce, then he catches with both hands, paying attention to his footwork, feeling the shoulders work, working both knees, and remembering what Coach MB said about tennis: Tennis is not a one-handed sport.

Today, Lester missed catching three out of seventy-five balls.

All three misses happened when Lester tried to catch one-handed.

PEP TALK FROM LESTER

PLAY OR DIE MEANS
EVEN IF YOU LOSE, KEEP PLAYING

Losing is an arbitrary numbers game. In a tournament with a 64 player draw, there is one winner. There are 63 losers.

In Senior Comp Doubles at the TCSP—eight old people still moving and still hitting on courts 5 and 6 at 8:15—you have better odds—four winners and only four losers.

Lester is human. He hates losing. Winning gives him a buzz. But losing makes him dig deep into his ancient rickety old man self.

Why did he lose? What can he do about it? He missed three backhand service returns. He hit two lobs long and two lobs short, giving the enemy net person two easy kills.

Losing is not dying.
Losing is a function of scoring.
Scoring is a set of rules.
Scoring forces you to strategize.
Strategizing is good for your brain.
Strategizing helps you to solve problems.
But even if you lost—the score was 4-6—you're still a

winner because you're still alive, still breathing, still hitting, still getting a buzz when you hit a clean shot, still able to climb the stairs to Willy's Café for a coffee, still able to take your place at the table with your tennis buds.

And even if you did lose, you still remember that one perfect shot, the sound of the ball on your strings, the arc of the ball, bright yellow against the green back-cloth at TCSP.

Hitting a clean winner is better than having your supposed winner returned, but if you love the arc of the ball connected to your racket which is connected through wrist and arm to shoulder and torque, which connects to the buzzing pleasure center in your brain—so what if you lose a couple points?

Lester loses a lot. Losing makes him sweat, makes him shake, makes him doubt himself.

But losing does not stop Lester from playing.

Aren't you out here on this magnificent court in all your tennis finery sweating and huffing alongside ancient people your own age because you don't want to die? Aren't you out here to move? Aren't you out here to work on your skills? Aren't you really here on this court to practice your new backhand half-volley so you can become a better doubles player? Aren't you here because you're alive?

Alive and not dead and planted six feet under?

THREE OLD TENNIS FRIENDS

Lester plays senior doubles with three older guys. Two are 87, one is 88. They love killing the ball. They hug the net, each one has a special shot.

Player JC, a PHD psychologist, poaches with great success. His weapon is this special Wilson racket with a monstrous oversize sweet spot. His special shot is the net kill. If you're receiving from the deuce court, J.C. kills your return with a lightning-fast forehand. An ex-fighter pilot, Player JC makes a confident enemy. You have two options.

Lob it over his head.

Or hit down his alley.

When he makes a good kill, you give him a thumbs up

❊ ❊ ❊

Player JK, a retired psychology professor, hits a mean whippy forehand. So you set him up, making sure the enemy hits to his forehands. Sometimes he kills better in the deuce-court, sometimes in the ad-court. His serve skims the tape because his toss is low. Tricky shot to return. When he double-faults, Lester makes sure to bump fists.

❊ ❊ ❊

Player BB, a hockey star in high school, comes to the court lugging his portable oxygen tank. Lester makes sure to check in with him before the match. Hey, BB, did you bring your atomizer? At 87, Player BB moves better than Lester does at 79, legs muscled like a high school jock. Player BB loves rushing the net, leaping, killing balls at head height. So when Lester partners with Player BB he sets him up for that rush-the-net shot with their code-word, which is *Mean-Face*. Before Lester serves, he checks with Player BB. "Hey, BB, you got your Mean Face on?" Big grin from Player BB. At that moment, they are a team. And good teams win doubles.

How long will they play?

When these three stop playing, Lester will feel very old.

He'll have to play ever smarter.

SMART SHOTS FOR SENIOR DOUBLES

1. The Senior Serve.

You want spin for control. You don't want a blooper, bopped into the court with the pancake grip. You want a shot you can practice on your own, by yourself.

When you deliver your serve into enemy territory, you don't have to run or beg your feet to cooperate with the knees, getting you into position. With a little pawing of the ground (think Rafa Nadal), you're already there—in the hitting zone.

Because you're standing still, you can focus on hitting your serve. Ball-toss, backswing, hit, follow-through. Take some lessons from your local pro. Or check out Tomaz on You Tube. Tomaz is a Slovenian tennis genius with a great sense of irony. Easy to follow drills. Just Google "Feel Tennis."

Practice your serve. Keep those double-faults down. Aiming the serve is more important than power. If you use the frying pan grip, you'll hit a flatter serve. Less spin, hard to control. A good pro can help you escape from the pitty-pat serve.

Try serving underhand.

P.S. If you're working out alone, add the Serve + One Exercise. This exercise forces you to change your focus. And maybe to change your grip.

Serve one ball with the second ball in your pocket.

Hit the serve, then hit the second ball.
Use a forehand then a backhand.

2-3. Bolster your strategy with Dropshots and Lobs.

Once you get the ball in play (serve), the next two most important shots for senior doubles are the dropshot and the lob. Both of them delivered with spin.

They go together.

On your first return of serve in senior doubles, try lobbing over the enemy net-person. Don't worry where the enemy net-person is standing. Hit your lob and force the enemy to play the first ball. Even if they win the point, you still made them work for it early in the play—that sets a good tempo right away. You did not hit the ball in the net, showing off your nerves. And losing the point after a short-court scuffle is better than losing the point on an out-ball, or a net-ball.

If the net-person crowds the net, you could win the point outright with your lob. Remember to use your legs. Lift that ball. If the net-person's speedy partner returns the lob, then you either hit another better lob or you bring out your dropshot. When Lester lobs, he adds slice. In his younger days, he hit topspin lobs—but that takes more energy—and you have to change your grip.

When the enemy starts to return your lob, try drop shotting your service return. Go cross-court, not down the line. Remember that the net is six inches lower at the strap. If the enemy net-person is fast, you might lose a point or two. But your goal in doubles is to force the enemy to change position. If you get a heap of spin on the drop-shot, your reward will be immediate enemy confusion.

The key to hitting a drop shot: stay with the ball longer. Pay attention to the meeting of ball and racket strings.

Is it an explosion? Or is the meeting a kiss?

4. Playing hard ball.

The next most important shot is the hard ball winner.

The hard ball winner could be a groundstroke or a volley. You use the hardball to win a point. To intimidate the enemy. To change the rhythm of play.

If your partner hugs the baseline—

If your partner loves to show off with the rally ball—

If your partner keeps hitting a perfectly stroked ball to the enemy net person—

If your partner deploys a singles rally ball strategy in a doubles match—

That's when you unsheathe the hard ball.

Rallying in doubles is certain death—it's too predictable, back and forth, high over the net, hard to change direction—and gives the enemy an easy poach.

Rallying keeps your team too close to the baseline.

In senior tennis, hugging the baseline is certain death.

To stop these baseline rallies, you whack the ball right at the enemy.

Go for the shoelaces, not the eye-glasses.

(The pros aim at the thigh, sometimes forcing the Toreador Defense—instant sideways stance, emulating the grace of the bull-fighter.)

If both enemy players are at the net, you slam your hard ball down the center of the court, forcing them to call for it—Mine! Yours!—and if they don't call for it, there's a good chance your hard ball will win the point.

5. The next most important shot is the volley.

The best volleys call for the ready position—hit from leg-strength—and a rigid forearm forming the magic L-shape with biceps and shoulder, guided by the perfect volley of Rod Laver (winner of two Grand Slams). Practice this pose in the mirror. The volley gets better if the racket face is eye-level with the volleyer, or close to it. The L-shape forces the volleyer to lower the Center of Gravity. Knees bent, feet apart, not a dignified look, but what do you care—you win the point. You impress the enemy players. For pictures of grips and angles on the racket face, You Tube Vic Braden—Tennis for the Future.

6. The Half-Volley.

This is the simplest shot in senior doubles. The ball comes right at your feet. You don't have to move. It helps to bend your knees, which lowers your COG (center of gravity). If the ball comes at you, use your backhand, two hands if you need to—and make sure your racket face is tilted back, not closed—you want the half-volley to clear the net. You can bunt the ball back over. You can hit a ton of slice, cradling the bottom of the ball. To keep your head clear in a match, you need to practice lots of half-volleys. Use the short court. Practice your spin-ball.

7. The best drill for senior doubles is short-court tennis.

Two players hit soft shots cross-court, ad court first. Your boundary is the service court. After you master cross-court, you practice hitting short down-the-line. The reason for soft shots: you have more control.

Softer is harder than hitting crazy-hard.

Hitting softer forces you to focus.

To succeed in short-court, you must get down to the ball. This drill improves your footwork.

8. Scoring short-court tennis.

If your senior brain needs the scoring ritual to maintain focus, you can play a game that ends when a player stacks up 15 points, Rules: no volleys, the ball must bounce on your court before you hit it. It's like ping-pong, all shots are ground-strokes.

9. Alternate serving.

Player One serves five. Player Two serves five. If you add a third player, you play two-against-one, rotating the serve every five points. When someone wins, then you rotate. Players A and C on one side of the net. Player B across from them.

Playing short-court forces you to study the ball, to lower your center of gravity. Studying the ball up close will make you a better senior, a better person.

10. Smarter Senior Doubles: Learn to operate from the Queen Spot.

Often, Lester partners with senior players who take up the wrong position on the doubles court.

Example: When their partner is receiving, they crowd the net, with one foot in the alley—forcing their partner to cover 87% of the court. Making it easy for the enemy to lob.

When their partner is <u>serving</u>, they crowd the net again, with one foot in the alley. Yes, they leave that same 87% wide open. Same truck lane down the middle, same ease of being lobbed over.

When they serve, they stand too close to the center line.

No angle from there. And too much open court to cover if the server tries to charge the net.

Often these Younger Seniors confuse doubles with singles —where they won by rallying from behind the baseline— big heavy booming loopers. When your partner displays this confusion, instead of watching this carnage, you need to hit a drop shot.

Or a sharp volley.

Or the high well-spun lob.

But when you have a doubles-savvy partner, the key to winning senior doubles is to set up early, and to understand the power of the Queen Spot. Christened by Coach MB, and named after the most powerful piece on the chessboard, the Queen Spot can re-boot your doubles game. An analogy lurks here: the Queen has the most power on the chessboard.

In tennis, the Queen is the brains of the doubles court.

One: Your partner is receiving from the deuce-court.
You're in the <u>neutral</u> Queen Spot, beside the service T where

the service line meets the center line. "Neutral" means you can intercept the cross-court service return.

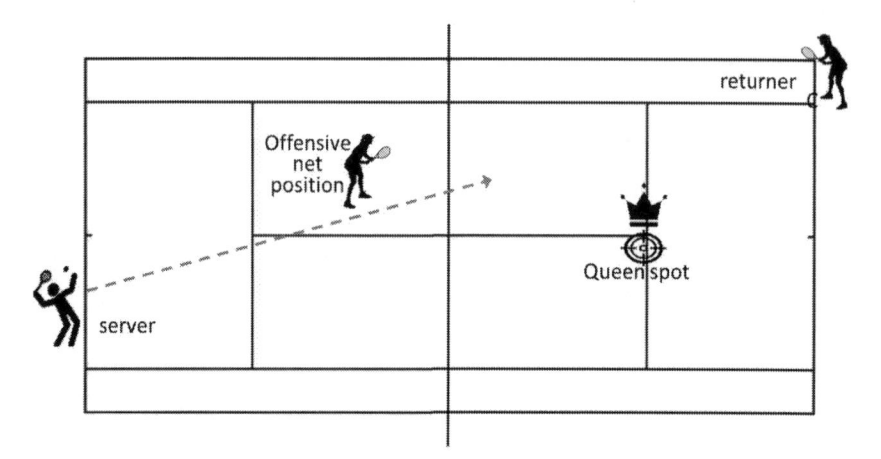

Note that on the server's side, the offensive net position is different: closer to the net and wider off the center line.

What comes next depends on your partner's service return. If it's flat and fast, you can assume that a hot, hard, bang-bang shot will be coming back your way. So advance, tracking the ball for a kill, to the <u>offensive</u> Queen Spot, a couple of feet up toward the net.

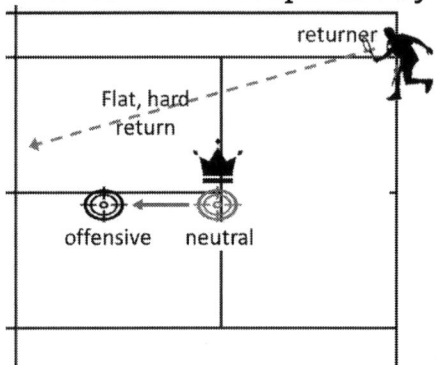

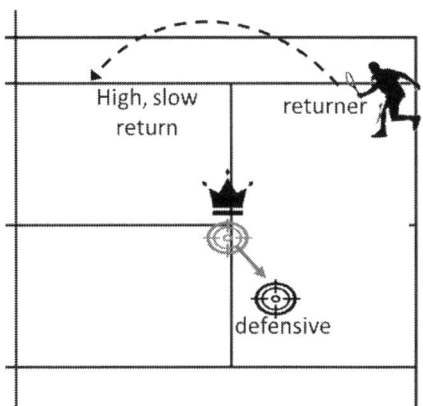

But if your partner's service return is a floater, retreat to the <u>defensive</u> Queen Spot, behind the service line and wide, closing off the enemy's cross-court winner.

In that defensive position, it's less likely that a lob can go over your head. Even if the enemy is allowed to advance, just move to the <u>defensive</u> Queen Spot and lower your COG (Center of Gravity) to be ready. You're still in the point. Call out "Mine" or "Yours," connecting with your partner. And isn't that one of the main reasons you play senior doubles? You're connected; you're not alone out there.

Two: The Queen must dance (and collect garbage)

Playing from the Queen Spot re-organizes your thinking, dragging your senior player-self up and away from the baseline, backing you off the net. But it's only the start of your dance as the net person on a tennis team. Start with the basic steps: neutral, offensive, defensive. If an incoming ball goes behind you to your partner, stay on neutral.

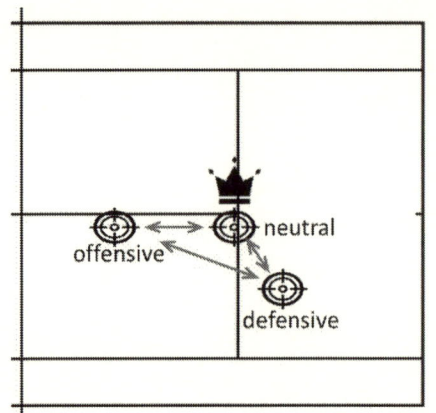

React to your partner's shot, since that sets up what you can expect for the next incoming ball. Your partner hits one low and fast: move up to the offensive spot. Slow and high: move back to be defensive, since the next ball coming in is likely to be unpleasant.

Keep moving. Watch your opponents for clues, for "tells" as to what they're going to hit.

- Forehand or backhand?
- How are the hips turned?
- Where are the feet moving?

Anticipation is all, especially for seniors. We don't move as fast others, so we have to learn to anticipate.

Feel free to move. There are no walls on a tennis court. That center line isn't a wall. Besides, walls don't work – not in Berlin or along the Rio Grande. So step across that center line to block or volley. Go with your momentum. Call "Mine!" and go for it.

Yes, the Queen is mighty and mobile. But it's also the Queen's job to collect the garbage. By garbage we mean any of those dinky balls that drop short on your team's side of the net. "But it's on my partner's side." No, it's yours, because you, the net person, are closer. Count the steps, you're closer than your partner. It's your job to get that ball, to collect the garbage.

Three: Seniors who have not had good doubles training often bring out their singles arsenal on the doubles court.

Here's one reason:

When they watch tennis on TV, seniors watch singles—that's what gets hyped on TV—two muscular youngsters (female or male) pounding big forehands cross-court. Pounding big backhands down the line.

The tennis players on TV are younger—they are decades distant from anyone over 65.

Seniors don't have that sort of muscle.

Seniors can't move that fast.

Seniors who stand close to the net are copying pro tennis as viewed on the TV—from the comfort of a Barcalounger.

Get out of your chair.

Get back on the court. If you are not serving or receiving, or your partner isn't serving, you occupy the Queen Spot. Back away from the net. Take up a position along the service line, with one foot close to the center line. Your opponents might give you looks. Smirks, even. But you have the training. You know where that ball is going. And you know where to stand, because for this moment you are in the Queen Spot—you have mastered the three-way dance.

Neutral.

Or Offensive.

Or Defensive.

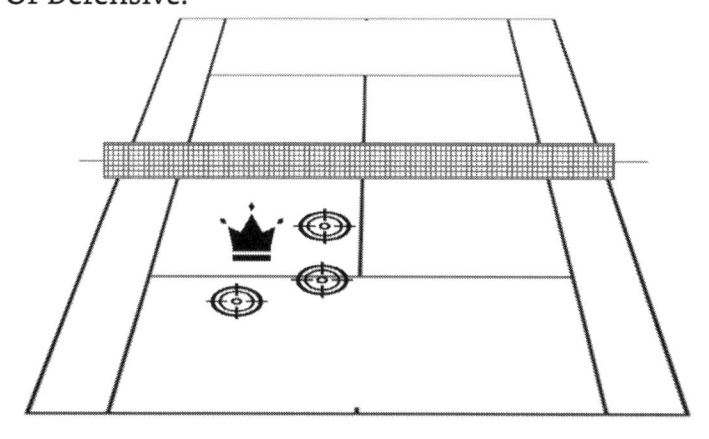

If you stay low, with your knees bent, you'll get your racket on more balls. You'll hit better volleys, and graceful half-volleys.

Fun on the court.

Play or die.

PART III

TENNIS INJURIES —GETTING HURT, GETTING WELL

HOW TO SURVIVE AND THRIVE IN COMP SENIOR DOUBLES

Comp Senior Doubles at the TCSP is open to any senior over 65. Seniors who are not dues-paying members are welcomed if they sign up with the Front Desk. These comped seniors bring good solid tennis to the courts, five days a week. They bring knowledge and skill—many of them are 3.5s—and they enjoy playing against other 3.5s. Playing with 3.5s forces Lester to work. He huffs and puffs. He sweats. He takes water breaks. He bites down on Kind Bars.

But he still can't run.

He's still late to the ball.

And he gets the fraternal smirk-eye when his slice cuts through the opposition.

On the battlefield of Comp Senior Doubles, Lester loses a lot. He loses more than he wins.

But playing against these guys—some of them are 15 years younger—tests Lester's mettle, and his shots. So when he hits a volley, he recalls all those volley-lessons—the most recent from Coach MB—the ready position, feet spread, knees bent to lower your COG, both hands on the racket.

These are great moments for an old guy. As he makes contact, Lester smiles, feeling the power transfer from his toes all the way up to ball contact. That solid sound makes his tennis rebirth worthwhile. And across the net, he hears the enemy talking.

Good player, that guy Elder.

Yes, his partner says. Still can't move.

Let's nail this guy anyway.

Okay, let's.

One A-Team player had a slice that was better (and smoother) than Lester's slice because he was younger, and his excellent footwork got him into position before he hit, his ball driving Lester sideways, hurting those knees. So the really tough shots in Comp Senior Doubles—good enemy opponents hit better than weak opponents—triggered Lester to confess his weak spots to Coach MB, who, like a magician, developed a drill to strengthen the weak spots.

Even though he was a thrifty guy, Lester didn't mind paying for lessons. Payment gave him access to an incredible resource—the tennis brain of Coach MB—but it also gave him 75 minutes of perfect on court practice—focus, teamwork, problem-solving, getting better at the game he loved.

Payment also took the guesswork out. The time he spent taking a lesson insulated Lester. For 70 minutes, Lester belonged here. This was his turf. After a long lay-off, Lester felt right at home.

❋ ❋ ❋

The control room for Senior Comp Doubles was the Front Desk. Sign-ups started at 9 AM on Saturday, often jamming the phone line, where Lester kept calling, dialing and re-dialing until the Front Desk answered—

Tennis Center Sand Point—how can I help you?

The players for the week showed up on a spread-sheet roster at the very bottom of the Adult column on the TCSP website, after you clicked Seniors and scrolled down and down and down to the very bottom. Two courts, five weekdays, Monday through Friday, eight players a day—several names unknown to Lester.

A list that was male-dominant.

Why did some women players avoid Comp Senior Doubles?

It didn't take long for Lester to figure out the answer to that question—it was buried in the social logistics of Comp Senior Doubles.

The heavy hitters took over Court 6, leaving Court 5 to the lesser hitters.

If there were five heavy hitters, the players on Court 6 often set up a rotation system that disrupted play on lesser Court 5. The lust to play on Court 6 helped Lester suffer his first sports injury at the TCSP.

SILENT SMIRKS AND BODY LANGUAGE: ANTICS OF THE A-TEAM

A chilly morning in February. Three normal regular average everyday non-A-Team senior players warming up on Court 5—Players JJ and AT—two women with big boomer forehands—and Lester.

But from Court 6 across the silken green divider mesh, Lester could hear the affected busyness of serious athletic male hustle—grunts, pops, shoe soles slapping the court, solid tennis footwork—old men trying to hit like young hotshots on the ATP Challenge Circuit.

Old men smirking like they were back in high school.

The time on the Clock said 8:18—only seven players had shown up—a senior player was 3 minutes late.

Lateness matters more when there is a strict enforced time limit for play. Because when the clock swarmed around to 9:25, and the buzzer sounded—it marked the end of complimentary tennis for that day.

At 8:22, the entry flap flew open and here came player number 8. A medium-sized senior male wearing studious matching warm-ups, blue with a white stripe-insignia that labeled the late newcomer as a serious player, serious enough to be A-Team.

Warm-Up Suit glanced away from Lester and his buds, awaiting his arrival on Court 5.

Lester said good morning.

But Warm-Up Suit did not reply with a hello. Or a good morning. Or even a quick look. Instead, he made a point of looking away from the obvious need of the threesome on Court 5. He held a steady course, away from Lester and Players DA and TW, crossing through the symbolic barrier netting onto Court 6, turning his attention onto the four A-Team players.

Warm-Up Suit's posture of certainty meant that he thought he belonged there, the Fifth Man, with the A-Team, on Court 6.

As if no other spot in the tennis universe existed at this moment—Court 6 was the Golden Bowl, the sacred turf.

* * *

Through the netting, Lester watched the foursome huddle together at the net strap for a serious discussion—how to play with five A-Team members on the same court. They were joined by Warm-Up Suit.

A minute or two in the huddle.

Mumbles, muffled guy talk, heads shaking, shoulder shrugs. One of the A-Teamers pointed at Court 5. As if to remind Warm-Up Suit—those poor guys on Court 5 need a fourth.

Warm-Up Suit rolled his eyes, shook his head.

His mouth hung on the edge of a sneer.

No way was this guy stepping onto Court 5, making a fourth for Lester's lonesome threesome, taking a long step down.

For Warm-Up Suit, it was A-Team or nothing.

* * *

The boys at the net finished their work and dispersed. Took their positions, four early A-Team guys winding up their warm-up, using their smooth strokes to re-define the turf of the A-Team, sacred and sacrosanct from 8:15 to 9:25.

Warm-Up Suit was red in the face. Anger spewed from his eyes. No one likes to be rejected. Because of Covid, there were no benches on any court, no chairs, no place to sit—a clear message from TCSP management: if you're not playing, vacate the court.

Warm-Up Suit had entered on the Court 5 side of the back wall. When he huffed his way to the exit, Warm-Up Suit was careful to stay on Court 6, all the way to the back wall.

From his point-of-view, Court 5 did not exist.

He pushed his way through the exit flap.

Gone.

Leaving Lester and his buds to play Australian, two against one—a good way to practice, a weird way to play—and keep score.

The singles guy serves.

The two-man team returns into the singles court. The doubles team has to hit singles targets—inside the doubles lanes The singles guy can hit into the whole doubles court. Lester had played good Australian when he was younger, before the bad knees, when he had mobility. Making full use of his spin serve and his disguised drop-shot, he had been competitive.

But today, alone on Court 5, Lester shuffled to the ball with medium pain. If he got to the ball in time, he went for a winner.

On the other side of the ball-netting, the A-Team gang on Court 6 played the perfect match. A solid thunking sound on the serve.

Quick well-modulated footwork on the net approach.

A healthy masculine grunt on the return.

All four players converging on the net.

Volley. Volley. Grunt. Volley. Grunt. Winner.

Silence.

Grins from the players, proud of their prowess as a quartet.

Proud of the skill of their opponents across the net.

The smallest movement expressed the presence of entitlement.

Lester looked at the clock.

Eleven minutes after nine.

Lester served, making sure he shifted his weight, trying to avoid the pain from the twisty sprain.

❋ ❋ ❋

As the clock hand hit nine-fifteen, Lester's knee wobbled. Twisted, forcing him to stop moving.

His shot went wide.

He lost the point.

The pain in his knee zapped down the fibula to the ankle, a javelin of electricity.

He shook his head.

There was still time on the clock, but he was done for the day.

Thanks to Covid, there was no place on the court for an old man with a wounded knee to sit down.

The closest seat was in Lester's car.

Lester apologized. His two Court 5 buddies asked if he was okay. They were trying to be nice. Trying not to be upset by the departure of Warm-Up Suit, the Eighth Man. Did they understand the magic pull of the closed circle that was Court 6?

As Lester limped off the court, the only sounds he heard were the wheezes and grunts from Court 6.

No question: these A-Team guys could play.

Stumbling along outside the shelter of TCSP, feeling the rain snap on his parka, Lester's analytical brain started in listing the Ifs.

If Lester had been a certified member of the A-Team, maybe things would have been different.

If he'd been recognized as a temporary A-Team, then Warm-Up Suit would have been happy to play on Court 5.

If there had been four guys on Court 5—giving Lester a partner who could run down those unreachable balls—then his knee would have been under less pressure.

Lester reminded himself—Complimentary Senior Tennis was not only free—it was also survival of the fittest.

If you were not fit to play, then you owed it to the others to get off the court.

Being old was not an excuse.

Being old was something to avoid.

Forget the wounded—leave them behind, and get on with your own game.

On your own court.

If you kept your head down, you could play forever.

Unless you had an injury.

And this particular injury would keep Lester off the courts for three weeks.

INJURED ATHLETE

The retreat from Court 5 to Lester's car was a nightmare trek through icy slanting rain. He wished for his cane. He needed a wheelchair.

But driving with the right leg felt crazy, useless, limp, pulsing with pain.

Lester made it home. Going into his house from the garage, he kept catching himself from falling by pushing against the brick wall.

He located his cane, a gift from his wife. He used the cane to move from the fridge—where he grabbed an ice-pack from the freezer—to get him down the hallway to the bedroom.

His wife was at her computer.

She asked if he was okay.

Twisted my ankle, he said.

Are you doing heat and ice? she said.

Just on the verge, he said.

RICE, his wife said.

Lester deployed the RICE defense.

R = rest.

I = ice.

C = compression.

E = elevation.

Using a bandana from the handkerchief drawer, Lester tied the ice-pack on his knee. The cold felt good.

Lying in bed, propped against pillows, Lester started the healing process by watching the Tennis Channel. It was late winter—the pros were playing in Rotterdam. The courts were green with white lines—easy to see the ball.

Would he ever play tennis again?

Using the cane, Lester was able to move around the house. The ice calmed the knee, but did nothing for the ankle. For lunch, Lester had soup and toast and a glass of wine that sent him back to bed for an afternoon nap. After the nap, Lester made it downstairs using the cane. He made two phone calls.

One to his alternative medicine guy, a chiropractor-naturopath. And the other on to the sports medicine clinic at UW-Med, with offices in the shadow of Husky Stadium.

※ ※ ※

To help bring down the inflammation while he waited for his appointments, Lester took a homeopathic remedy called Calc. Fluor. Little white pills, purchased by mail-order from a supplier in Los Angeles. To help diminish the swelling in his leg, Lester took Kali Muriaticum, more white pills.

To treat the injury, Lester chose Arnica.

What is Arnica?

Let us explore.

If you check out Arnica on Amazon, you wind up on a page that shares Arnica with Voltaren. These two pain-whackers have emerged onto the computer screen after years in the shadowy half-dark between Medicine with a Capital M and the twin opathies—Naturopathy, which once was taboo in America—and Homeopathy, which has its own magic.

Homeopathic remedies are super-mild.

Unlike the dangerous opioid outflow from Big Pharma (fentanyl, oxycodone, Oxycontin, hydrocodone, codeine, morphine, etc.)—where an overdose can kill you—just a pinch of a tiny pill from Homeopathy can help you get through to the next tennis game.

The pills work best dissolved under the tongue—that way they don't have to go through the digestive tract—and you'll need to do some reading. There are two classic texts—both well-dated and heavily-thumbed:

J.T. Kent's *Repertory of the Homeopathic Materia Medica* (weighs 2.5 lbs.).

William Boericke's *Pocket Manual of Homeopathic Materia Medica* (weighs 12 oz.).

❋ ❋ ❋

In the late 19th century, while the AMA sabotaged homeopathy, women medics surged ahead. Here's the dean of homeopathy in America, Dana Ullman: "The first women's medical college in the world was the homeopathic Boston Female Medical College, founded in 1848. Four years later it became the New England Female Medical College, and in 1873, it merged with Boston University, another homeopathic college. Homeopaths also admitted women physicians into their national organization considerably before orthodox physicians did. Homeopaths admitted women into the American Institute of Homeopathy in 1871, while women were not invited into the A.M.A. until 1915. (43) The orthodox medical school at Johns Hopkins finally agreed to accept women students as late as 1890, but not out of interests in women's rights. They were offered a $500,000 endowment."

(Find this Online, from *A Condensed History of Homeopathy*, by Dana Ullman MPH, who is one smart dude.)

For his combined knee-ankle injuries, Lester took his remedies 3-4 times a day. Arnica 30c for the shock. Ferrum Phos 6x for the inflammation. Picric Acid 30c for weakness. He knew the remedies were working because he started feeling better. When the healing process leveled off, Lester started exercising, attaching his ankle to a stretch band attached to a hook in the door jamb.

* * *

It was hard to see a doctor—they were busy with the Covid—but Lester finally got in to see a Sports Medicine specialist, where he learned about an injection called Visco Supplementation. The doctor said it would last maybe six months. Lester's knees had already tried cortisone—it lasted for two weeks—but this Visco sounded better than PRP (a whirlybird blood plasma mixture).

Lester was ready to go.

But first he had six visits with a physical trainer (she possessed a PHD), who helped his legs get stronger. Before he exercised, the trainer worked over his kneecap with experienced fingers.

In between visits to the trainer, Lester got adjustments from his natural medicine guy—a chiropractor-naturopath—who helped Lester with balance and stamina.

* * *

Lester also turned to the computer screen, where he found two physical trainers—Bob and Brad—broadcasting from the American Midwest, who had produced a 10 minute YouTube session on the fibula.

Lester watched it seven times.

He took notes.

These two trainers made funny jokes, funny teetering on the edge of cornball.

A footnote at the bottom of the screen said that their program gained umpteen viewers every day.

To demonstrate the diagnosis of the day, they deployed a plastic skeleton. For the fibula they pointed to a narrow bone on the outside of the skeleton's leg, running from the ankle to the knee.

If you had an injury, they said, the first action was to control the heat, the inflammation that swells up.

Ice.

Lester thought he was done with the ice, but he felt better when he strapped on an ice-pack.

The ice-pack made him feel like he was taking action.

The next day, Lester followed Bob and Brad as they demonstrated the Alphabet Exercise for the ankle and the foot.

While sitting down, Lester flexed both ankle and foot—rotating to form the capital letter A. He was doing the alphabet again. He felt guilty for not having done it every day. Lester was not perfect. He hated admitting that.

Then capital Letter B.

Then capital letter C.

On through the alphabet, feeling no pain because he was being careful, Lester rotated.

His right foot bent forward.

Then backward.

For the letter H, his big right toe made a vertical line, then crossed to make the straight line, then moved from high to low to make the closing vertical line on the right.

※ ※ ※

Lester felt clumsy.

He figured it out: the reason for making the alphabet, all 26 letters, was more psychological than tactical—it kept Lester going when he was eager to stop.

His wife asked what he was doing. She was here to make sure he was okay. Lester was on the sofa in front of the basement TV, watching doubles on the Tennis Channel, his right foot drawing the letters of the alphabet in the air.

What are you doing? she said.

The alphabet, he said.

What letter are you on? she said.

Can't you tell? —I'm on the letter W.

I've done that exercise, she said. And that's not what the Letter W looks like.

Okay, Lester said. Lemme try again.

What are you watching? she said.

Men's Doubles, he said. From Rotterdam.

That's a beautiful green, she said. On the screen, I mean.

Easy to see the ball, he said. Against that background.

When is your appointment with the doctor?

Tomorrow, eight o'clock.

I'm eager for you to see him, she said.

Me, too.

I'm liking it that he's a real doctor, she said. And not one of your favorite pathics.

I'll let him know, Lester said.

When you see him, make sure to ask about that Alphabet thing, okay?

FIVE WOUNDED SENIORS

In senior tennis, bad knees is like a special club—old people with joint problems that affect their tennis—and Lester persuaded a cadre of tennis friends to write about their experience with bad knees.

1. Player BS had one knee replaced and is waiting to do knee number two.
2. Player RAM has knee pains and wears a brace.
3. Player BG has knee pains and keeps checking with her doctors.
4. Player LP has discovered a miraculous ankle brace—expensive, but worth a read-through—it also helps knees.
5. Player JJ had surgery and got right back onto the court.

***

1. Knee Replacement By Player BS

I have a long relationship with tennis. My childhood summers were spent at various day camps and junior tennis programs. My parents were both avid players so there was lots of family tennis. However not being particularly athletic my game never rose above the level of a mediocre recreational player. Competitive tennis was not for me.

As an adult I went through phases of playing or not depending on other interests and available partners. I hardly played at all for the first decade and a half of the 2000s. Then as retirement approached my interest rekindled and I started playing two or three times a week.

Then my knees starting hurting. I tried various braces and over the counter pain meds. My doctor suggested diclophenac gel (Voltaren) which helped for a while. X-rays showed almost no cartilage left in either knee. Eventually walking, standing, or sitting for any length of time was hard to bear. Ironically my knees didn't hurt that much while playing tennis. Adrenalin is a great drug. But occasionally a misstep would twist my knee. I was starting have trouble covering the court. I could still get to most shots but it was difficult to stop, turn around and recover back to the center of the court.

So I started thinking about having one or both knees replaced. Many of my friends had had knee replacements and swore by them. My wife has had both hips replaced and is much happier for it. I found an orthopedic surgeon I liked and got on his schedule. Surgery was to be late February which would leave me March and April to recover ready for outdoor tennis in May.

The operation itself went well and my convalescence was not too bad. Ice and over the counter pills kept the pain at bay. I was religious about doing my stretching exercises and my range of motion improved rapidly. Ten days after surgery I was even able to walk the two blocks to a neighborhood physical therapist.

Then covid complicated things. The therapist had to close his office as part of the initial lock down, but I continued to improve by following the exercise program he had given me on my own. By late April I was walking well and ready to start playing doubles. My doctor said I was way ahead of the curve and I was pretty happy. However no tennis. Not that I wasn't ready to play. There just weren't any open courts. So I got an extra month and a half of convalescence until the parks department decided it was safe to open the courts.

I was very happy to be playing tennis again. My mobility was greatly improved although my new knee was still pretty sore. Oddly my other knee, the left, felt great. It had been almost as painful as the right and I had initially thought I'd have it replaced immediately afterward. Hard to say if this was due to the extra time off or just better overall stability from the right.

That was 18 months ago. My right knee is still quite painful. Probably more so than it was a year ago. My doctor says sometimes that happens. The surgery is structurally successful but doesn't eliminate all the inflammation and there is really not anything he can do to make it better. My left knee is deteriorating. I move only about as well as I was before the surgery.

So I have to decide if I want to have more surgery. I am not eager to go through the hospitalization and recovery, especially if I end up with a new left knee that feels like my right one does now. Chances are I was just unlucky and my result will be better the second time but still. So I am looking for a second opinion and biding my time until hospitals aren't full of covid patients. Hopefully I won't have to limit my tennis in the meantime.

* * *

2: My Experience as a Senior Tennis Player By Player RAM

I took up tennis after a 50+ year hiatus because I had always loved playing the game as a young girl. The outdoor courts in my small, Midwestern town were free, and there was not much else to do. Once I left the Midwest, I never played again until an indoor tennis facility in Seattle was constructed within a short drive from my home, about 5 years ago. At the time of its construction, I had just retired, and had spare time to fill.

Ironically, when I registered as a new member of the facility, I never intended to become a good player. Instead, I was far more interested in the social benefits of playing tennis, including finding kindred spirits to replace career colleagues. I also intended to play tennis as a form of exercise that would help me fight the gradual progression of my osteopoenia.

I was soon discouraged. Not because of my skill level, but because, for the first time in my life, acceptance was illusory. Outside of tennis, being "nice" or "smart" or "funny" was enough. But in the tennis context, more was expected. I soon discovered that "kindred spirits" were serious about constantly improving their skills. In the blink of an eye, so was I. That task proved much, much harder than any undertaking I had previously attempted, including the practice of law.

The paradox of senior tennis is that short term memory begins to fail after 60, and senior tennis requires members to be 65 to be eligible. By definition then, seniors are doomed to forget not only the score, but more essentially, much of the skill development they learn. Ask a senior which grip they should use to serve, and they will likely not be able to tell you the name of it, although they will happily show you how they grip their racket during a serve.

So, a challenge unique to seniors is how to develop essential skills, given their memory shortcomings. Having studied for the 3-day Bar Exam in Washington State, I have some familiarity with memory exhaustion and useful tricks to maximize memory. Engaging both the left (analytical) and the right (creative) sides of the brain is essential. In the case of studying for the bar, extensive use of colored markers in preparing study cards helps train the right side of the brain to recall essential legal material. For example, the right side of the brain may vividly recall rainbow colored lists, such as the 7 elements of Adverse Possession in Property Law long after the left brain has collapsed while analyzing Article 9 of the Uniform Commercial Code.

Similarly, in tennis, the use of metaphors powerfully engages the right brain to imagine the required movement. For example, a racket motion and angle can be described as "giving Johnny a quick swat on the butt" or as "carrying a tray of wine," instantly triggering motor memory, rather than cerebral memory, to recognize the angle, motion, and strength required to perform the skill.

In addition to the use of metaphors as a memory device, a second useful tool for seniors is to anticipate, rather than react, to the direction, angle, and spin of the ball. It is well known from automobile accident analysis that seniors have diminished reaction time. This is just as true in tennis, as it is in driving. A core skill for seniors, then, is to develop an intense focus on the ball, as it is hit by the opponent, more than focusing on the ball after it crosses the net, or the place where the ball lands in the opponents court. Ask any senior what they need to do immediately after serving a soft serve and they will tell you that they need to come forward in anticipation of the return.

Last, but not least, seniors need to understand that they are no longer going to have the speed they used to have to come to the service line from the base line after a serve. Instead, a savvy senior will take a single step forward after serving, gradually covering the distance to the service line with each subsequent volley. "No Man's Land" (i.e., the space approximately 5' in front of the base line) is a senior's home.

I have been most fortunate to have a brilliant coach at TCSP who understands the limitations of seniors and who provides the work around solutions described above. Even better, I have also been extremely fortunate to discover that, in the process of improving my tennis skills, my bone density has also improved. My doctor directly attributes this improvement to tennis, showing me studies that indicated that tennis is the number one exercise to improve bone density. In other words, that kind of improvement just doesn't happen in golf!!

. . . .

3. Late Bloomer By Player BG

When I turned 40 and was a newly-minted lawyer, I decided to take up tennis as a sport that provided good exercise and the prospect of play for the rest of my life.

I had hit a tennis ball now and again, but I wouldn't call it "playing." So I enrolled in classes at the local park and began to learn to play. I'm now 80 and "the rest of my life" seems much shorter than it did. And it began to seem very short in mid-2020, when bursitis in both hips and SI joint pain in the low back began to plague me. By early 2021, all the pain was so severe that I all but stopped playing tennis altogether.

I have other hobbies: cooking, reading, sewing, so I was able to fill the time without missing tennis too much, and I walked the streets for exercise several miles several times a week, but I found that even that was painful afterward. Bursitis has recurred several times over the past 20 years or so, but never as bad as the past year. I was determined to heal myself with stretching and over-the-counter drugs, e.g., acetaminophen, but nothing gave more than very short-relief.

I finally bit the bullet and saw my orthopedic specialist for steroid injections to treat the hip bursa on both sides January 28, and it was miraculous! All pain GONE within 48 hours! I'll never make the mistake of waiting again!

According to the doctor, I can get these injections every three months, if necessary, without ill effects. That's good news. More good news is that I have no arthritis in my hips, so hip replacement(s) is not in the picture (yet). I was completely pain-free for about two weeks, when I went to the first tennis clinic in over a year. My low back was a bit painful afterward and more so after the second clinic a week later. I've now been on my feet a lot for the past several days in a sewing workshop, and my low back is quite sore.

When I went for the injections, my doctor's PA mentioned that if the low back pain returned quickly, I should consider having a back evaluation. I plan to do that in the very near future, if the current discomfort doesn't go away quickly. Steroid injections similar to those for the hips may be available for the back.

In the meantime, I'll continue to attend a tennis clinic available locally at a public tennis facility, and I'll rest on other days. My game has fallen off considerably this year, but it could be worse! One of the "costs" of the inactivity is that I've got no "legs!" I'm much slower than before 2020 and am having problems with quick changes of *direction.*

I've decided to just relax about all this, try to get back to yoga classes, and walk. My tennis game is not likely to improve much in the future, but I plan to enjoy playing without a lot of self-imposed pressure!

❋ ❋ ❋

4. Miracle Ankle Brace By Player LP

Player LP's best tennis shot is her lob. Deadly accuracy is an understatement—she can put that lob on a dime. She has a fascinating tale about her ankle brace. She is another one of Lester's attorney friends.

I am 76 years old. I started playing tennis when I was 65. So unlike most of my tennis peers, I do not have the frustration of declining abilities after a lifetime of tennis play. I am still improving. Or I was, until 50-year old multiple fractures to my left leg and ankle came back to bite me. My leg has never been right since the ski accident, but I've always been able to cope — until I couldn't anymore. With arthritis in the mix with the fractures, my ankle didn't bend and was very painful and always swollen. I tried it all — ice, heat, acupuncture, pain pills, and cortisone shots, which worked for awhile, and then didn't anymore. In the meantime, on the tennis court I learned not to chase the ball very far because it hurt too bad. Which of course wasn't exactly making me a great player.

Two years ago, after a winter on the beach in southern Mexico, where walking on the beach was crippling, I promised my friends when I got home I would get a second opinion about what could be done. (According to my doctors, surgery was not an option because of my age). With a bit of research, I discovered an orthopedic clinic dedicated to ankle and feet injuries at the University of Washington. The doctor reviewed my X-rays, watched me walk, examined me — and asked whether I had ever considered an ExoSym. I didn't know what he was talking about. He brought in his laptop and showed *me what it was, I agreed to pursue it, and off I went on an exciting journey to give me mobility for life. I did this not just for tennis, but to be able to walk the golf course, walk my dog, and just live life without pain.*

I was very lucky. The prosthetist who invented and patented the ExoSym has a clinic in Gig Harbor, an easy drive from Seattle where I lived. People come from all over the world to have an ExoSym made for them and to be trained to walk with it. With it I am bionic — a carbon fiber foot attached to carbon fiber struts up the back of my leg. My ankle and lower leg are stabilized and unable to move, thus protecting me from pain. After 8 weeks of fitting and training, I went right back onto the tennis court.

I know people who don't know me think "Oh my God, she's crippled and she's going to play tennis?" But really, I'm able to. My biggest problem has been convincing my mind that I can now chase the ball without hurting myself. And ExoSym wearers say movement will get easier with years of practice, so I'm looking forward to a long time playing tennis.

❋ ❋ ❋

5. Three Sport Wonder By Player JJ

Player JJ is 92.

She plays three sports.

One paddle sport, pickleball.

And two racket sports, badminton and tennis.

Her key word is "enjoy."

In 1998, Player JJ and her late husband Don brought the qualifying games for National Senior Games to Washington, her home state. (She said she was tired of traveling a long way to qualify.)

In 2013, she persuaded the bigwigs of National Senior Games to include pickleball.

For the 2022 games, participation of tennis players in the

National Senior Games will be capped at 900.

For the last three decades (except for 1991, surgery and recuperation), Player JJ has won at least one gold medal in one of her three sports.

Her surgeries include: right foot, both knees, two knee replacements, frozen left shoulder, two rotator cuff procedures, one hernia, a broken wrist, broken elbow, broken upper arm, and a cataract.

Player JJ played badminton growing up—she had wins over the boys in her high school, but she couldn't beat her future husband, Don, so she married him.

Their marriage lasted for 70 years. When Player JJ was 42, she and her husband joined with another couple to buy a tennis club. About learning tennis: "We decided if we were going to own a tennis club, then we should probably learn how to play it."

About pickleballl: "Almost anyone can just go out and enjoy it right off the bat."

About having fun: "I have enjoyed myself my whole life doing what I do."

❋ ❋ ❋

Here's Player JJ, in her own voice—her subject is rushing the net.

I played in the National 90+ Claycourt Tennis Championships in Houston in September 2021. I won the Ladies Doubles, but lost in the Singles finals. I had my knee replaced 20 years ago, and my doctor said I should just play singles or doubles, and not both, if I wanted to keep playing forever. I chose Doubles and didn't play singles until this Nationals. I enjoyed it and discovered that I could play in both without suffering from exhaustion.

I decided to play in the Singles in the National 90+ Grass Championships last week (December) also. I played the same player in the Singles finals who beat me on Clay 3 months earlier. I served and volleyed EVERY point. I saw a lot of passing shots go by me, right and left, but I knew if I didn't come in, I'd lose, because she had such a great drop shot.

I won the first set, but we had so many deuce games that I was getting really tired. I was ahead 6-5, serving for the match. We must have had a dozen deuces. I finally won the match 7-5. But on the final point, I went for an impossible shot, returned it, but twisted my wrist, and dropped my racket. If I had missed that shot, I couldn't have played another point. I would have had to default!

This was the first time I'd played on grass in 8 years. It was my first Nationals Singles Gold Ball! I've won 18 Doubles Gold Balls, but no singles! Very exciting win! I was scheduled to play in the Pickleball Nationals 3 days later. I went to Urgent Care. They took X-rays, which showed nothing was broken. He said that it was swollen because I had pulled a couple ligaments and sprained my wrist. His recommendation was not to use it for seven to 10 days, but he recognized me as a competitive athlete, and was sure I wouldn't listen to his advice. Boy, did he have me pegged!

I iced and heated it faithfully for the next three days. It was too painful to play singles, but I didn't want to let my mixed partner down, so I tried playing, but it was impossible. But I had a great time anyway. I met a great many old friends, and made a lot more new ones. I got to watch friends play more than I could have if I were playing myself. Now, I am doing what the doctor advised, and resting it for 7- 10 days. Maybe more since I'm sure I irritated it and made it worse!

Player JJ, 92 years old.

PART IV

SURVIVAL SKILLS FOR A NON-JOCK TRAPPED IN THE MANLY STATE OF TEXAS

LESTER'S FIRST A-TEAM

On a chilly Amarillo autumn afternoon, on the extra-ample grassy upper-class side-lawn of an Amarillo rich kid and fellow-Wolflin-School chum, Sammy D., Lester San Marino, eleven years old, offered up his fragile near-sighted boy-body to the fickle gods of team sports, worshipped by optimistic lads lusting to become the sports heroes of their time—lured by the high-value status of pro athletes—using the playing fields available to sixth-graders on the slippery cusp of pre-adolescence.

Lester was no good at touch football—too slow, too chicken, frozen reflexes, no grasp of team unity, his hands too small for the ball—but he was trying to perform, be one of the guys, be admitted to the magic circle of team sports, and he had just caught the ball and was wondering what comes next, what to do now, run or toss or fall down and surrender—and then he was down on the grass, surrounded by a ring of boy-faces, boy mouths yawping.

Lester lost his glasses.

He rolled over, got to one knee, tried to get to his feet.

The pain chiseled into his ankle, zipped up the outside bone, straight to the knee.

Lester could not stand up.

He could not walk.

He hated these group melees.

Someone handed him his glasses. Someone called Lester's Mom. He rode back home in the family Dodge, his face grey with failure. His Mom helped him to his bedroom. He felt safe there. When he went down the hallway to the bathroom, Lester hobbled along, pushing against the wall to take the weight off the injured leg.

* * *

Because of his injury in sixth-grade touch football, Lester spent two weeks on crutches.

He hated being a cripple.

In the hallway at Wolflin School, his fellow-students stared at him, then looked away.

Being a cripple meant you were a weakie.

Being a weakie made you an outcast.

He took forever going up a short flight of stairs.

No more touch football—where the simple word *touch* mutated into a tackle or a body-block.

Who cares about sports, anyway?

Then one Friday afternoon.

The school day was over.

The wind came swooping down from Colorado, Canada, Alaska, the North Pole. Lester had lingered, talking with a teacher about *The Call of the Wild*, a Jack London book—about a dog named Buck who goes on the hero's journey—from civilization back to the wilderness, where he finds his true calling—leader of a wolf pack.

Lester was eleven years old, forced to walk with a cane. Next year he would move from Wolflin School to Elizabeth Nixon Junior High, a long bike ride from Hughes Street. Lester liked progress, but he was torn about leaving Wolflin School—he loved the familiar, he didn't like change—untold unknowns waited in the darkness up ahead—and there was this beautiful teacher with auburn hair and Lester was in love.

Schoolboy crush, bud.

Snap out of it.

So another wintry North Texas afternoon, a cold dry wind—another grey Amarillo day—Lester all bundled up in his parka, two weeks into his sprained ankle and still using the cane, and home was a painful two blocks away.

Lester was limping away from Wolflin School, heading due south on Hughes Street, the cane tapping away, each painful step reminding him of his fall on the grassy field of sixth-grade touch football, when he heard fast feet scuffling.

* * *

The bump-bounce of a basketball on hard cold concrete.

The healthy exhalations of schoolboys working out.

Alone on the pale grey sidewalk, looking across the chilly autumnal playfield, Lester saw four guys weaving a drill with a basketball.

He knew these guys.

James C and Dale M and Rex B and Jimmy H.

Four guys from Lester's sixth-grade class, two in their shirtsleeves, the other two in T-shirts, jackets on the ground. As if this meeting was a spontaneous gathering of boyhood greats. Like a cosmic coincidence, four guys—the best athletes in Lester's small inchoate world—just happened to drop by the parched school playground after hours where a benign sports deity supplied a basketball and there was the rusty backboard—and now Lester stood outside their enviable athlete's circle watching them weave their elaborate dance on the gritty whitish-grey grade-school playground.

He knew he didn't belong in their company—no way could he move like that. No way could he pass like that. Or dribble. Or shoot. Or anticipate.

But he could watch, filled with a growing envy, as player A dribbled, passed to Player B, who cut behind Player C, passing the ball to Player D, who shot, a perfect slow-motion arc that ended when the ball dropped through a rusted metal hoop screwed onto an ancient backboard blasted by wind and rain. He felt left out.

Lester was freezing. He huddled inside his parka. His heart thudded—he knew all of these guys. They had value. In their bones, they understood teamwork.

One dribble, one bounce, one pass, another.

Shooting the ball to the next player.

Who was already moving, as if he could, by divine intervention, anticipate where this singular bounced ball would end up, passed to him chest-high, just right for grabbing, his inherited expertise allowing his body to leap off the gritty pavement of the school playfield at Wolflin School in late November in Amarillo, Texas.

To shoot.

To score.

While Lester was freezing, these efficient boy-athletes did not seem to feel the cold.

They focused on one thing—the ball.

Keeping the drill going.

Passing the ball in the air.

Bouncing the ball, ignoring the playfield grit.

Transforming the gritty playground into a magic palace of sport.

They drilled with one obvious goal—keep the play going by helping the other guy.

It was a total sporting moment without the need for scoring.

Godlike sporty team-work.

No losers, every guy a winner.

And Lester was shut out—he lacked the graceful agility, the rhythmic drill prowess that turned these ordinary boys into sports gods.

* * *

Because of their unique skill-level, they could work together as a team. They could dribble. They could pass. They could shoot. They could see two plays ahead, three, maybe four. Their boy-bodies were linked up with the algorithm of game-playing—what would happen next, what moves needed to be made to keep the drill going.

And Lester was envious.

Sad.

Short-changed by the universe.

Later in life, when Lester was chugging away in graduate school, he heard that two of these boys had become professional athletes in their chosen sports.

Football for Jimmy H.

Golf for Rex B.

Lester remembered not being surprised.

Remembering that cold grey day in November, he knew that these boys, guys in his school, in his homeroom, they came from a different planet.

Gifted. Cool.

They operated on a secret super-charged wave-length.

They possessed superior reflexes.

Superior eyesight.

They were drilling like professionals.

The four horsemen.

The four musketeers.

Held together by skill.

They were the A-Team of Wolflin School.

In society, their value was enhanced by sports.

How had they known about this sacred place? How had they arrived there at the same time equipped with a basketball? How did they know where to move? When to pass? When to shoot?

Lester was baffled.

He was envious.

Feeling a lump in his throat, Lester turned away from the A-Team and headed for home.

Was this the only A-Team in existence?

And what did Lester have to do to create his own A-Team equivalent.

LESTER DISCOVERS SPIN IN SPORTS

Haunted by the unattainable magic of the A-Team—instant brotherhood, enviable camaraderie, mystery of the genes, magic of the closed circle—Lester hauled his interest in writing to his first class in journalism.

It was senior year. Next year was college. When the journalism teacher learned that Lester was on the tennis team, he displayed a toothy ironic grin. With his Texas twang and a wise-ass French accent, the Journalism teacher appointed Lester *Le Rédacteur en chef du sports.*

The Editor of Sport for the weekly paper—*The Golden Sandstorm*—published on Friday—which meant, in any Texas town, the princely quasi-religious group ritual of high-school football.

So on alternate Friday nights, when the football team played its home-games, Lester perched on a hard wooden chair in the fancy glassed-in press box at the new Dick Bivins Stadium, in the midst of stern-faced football coaches, trying to discern, in the furious and nonsensical mayhem below, any traces of the talent of the ever-magical and always mysterious A-Team, those Wolflin School sixth graders.

Lester knew zip about football—a burst of action followed by flags from the referees and huddles on the grass amidst a myriad of multiple mind-numbing time-outs—ten minutes for the cheerleaders to shine. But Lester was interested because the head quarterback that year was also the captain of the tennis team, the talented Player DK—fast, agile, smart.

Player DK called the plays. He ran the ball. He was fearless. A bona fide jock. The crowd loved him. What could Lester learn from this guy?

On Friday night, Lester tracked the moves—and the athletic jock magic—of Player DK.

* * *

Football guys who won on Friday nights were high-school heroes on Monday. They were burly and hard, eager to display their body-builder muscles—thick necks, gorilla legs, body-blocking lesser mortals bumping thickish torsos and thighs, bumping students aside in the nervous high school hallway—but on Friday game-nights they looked different down there on the pale green gridiron under the sharp lights that chopped away the shadows.

They looked smaller.

Lester was searching for an insight into the game of football. It was brutal. It was dirty. Even if you were on the team, you might not get to play.

On the last game of the season, the Sandies worked their way to a tie—twelve to twelve on the scoreboard.

A long way to the finish line.

The clock ticked toward the final buzzer.

On the last play before the clock ran out, Player DK took the ball from the center, faked a pass, and then started running, tucking the ball under one arm, until he reached a pre-ordained spot on the grass, where he launched the ball, a spiral spinner, arcing down the field, where it was caught by a team-mate.

Who had not been at that spot when Player DK was running.

Who had materialized on that spot just in time to catch the

ball.

That intersection of player and football was filled with magic.

Sitting at his typewriter, Lester wrote the story of the Friday night game. He opened with short sentences, naming the key players—football guys liked seeing their names in print—and then he used three key words— "spiral" and "spinning" and "rotation"—stoking his writer's brain so that he could end his write-up with the flair of one long sentence:

"At the climax of four breathless quarters—with 301 yards through the air and 292 on the ground—as the football chronometer ticked towards a symbolic doomsday loss, the stalwart AHS defenders of Amarillo's historic pigskin trophy teetered on the brink of defeat, but not without triggering the battle-savvy brain of the steely Sandstorm Quarterback, Player DK, who called for a Quarterback Sneak, exposing himself and his bones to the blunt bludgeons of the opposition, brutes to the core, and then the maneuver, replayed in slow-motion, as Player DK, the team captain, and its brightest star in decades, rammed through the opposition's line, fighting off a bevy of enemy players for two full furlongs before loosing the spinning spiral pigskin, rotating in the crisp autumn air with a majestic torque, shunting the ball into the hands of his worthy second-in-command, Player RD, a fleet runner, perhaps the speediest athlete on this year's Sandie gridiron squad, who appeared at the precise second—the pre-ordained target for the knowledgeable arm of Player DK, tucking the ball under his wing before sprinting his way to glory, billowed by the cheers of the loyal fans of our own AHS, safe in the stands, above the bloody fray."

※ ※ ※

Was Lester writing to probe the A-Team experience on the football field? Did those beefy fellows have that feeling of divine A-team-esque togetherness as they ran a play? Was that what the fans cheered for?

Lester did not realize he was also writing to explore the ubiquity of spin until he saw his write-up in print, a cold Friday morning, wind from the north, with snow in the weather forecast, Lester reading his sentences in the journalism office.

But his football piece focused on the precise connection between passer and receiver. The quarterback threw to an empty hole downfield, repeating a drill from practice, and if the drill worked with the pressure of game-time play, the hole would be filled by an alert receiver.

That was a pure two-man A-Team in action.

Hypnotic, musical, choreographed.

Made possible by the spin on the ball.

Spin that caught Lester's attention.

He was aware of spin that he put on the tennis ball—he was late, lousy footwork—but to study spin on the football he needed to do some research—which started with the personal library of the football coach, himself a student of football, who lent Lester a book on the history of football.

From the book, Lester learned that the forward pass launched by Player DK in the 1950's had come into the game around 1907. The team that turned the forward pass into a weapon were the American Indian footballers from a school called Carlisle. The shot was called an overhand spiral. The Coach was Glenn Scobey (Pop) Warner. One of his players was Jim Thorpe, the legendary Olympic athlete. Carlisle beat Penn. They beat Princeton.

And all because of the spin that controlled the flight of the ball.

❋ ❋ ❋

Lester was curious about technique.
About spin in sports.
Which no one talked about.

Was spin so obvious to players and coaches and sports reporters that it was a given?

If Player DK could spin a football, then Lester could focus even more on spinning a tennis ball.

And then he read Tilden's book, *Match Play and the Spin of the Ball*, and even though Tilden was right-handed, Lester now had a mandate to keep on chugging with spin.

And then, the school year was over. Lester was grooming a neighborhood guy to take over his paper-route. Three weeks before he was to leave town, Lester saw another angle to amateur tennis.

The invasion of the Golden Boy.

A tennis player Lester's age who understood the role of spin in tennis.

THE DEFINITION OF STATUS

A GOLDEN BOY WIELDING A MAGICAL SLICE BACKHAND

Late Amarillo Summer, yellow leaves drifting down, autumn in the air. Lester and his high-school tennis pal, Player RW, hitting on Court 3 at Ellwood Park.

A black limo parks at the curb. The driver, a guy in a suit, opens the back door and a blonde player emerges.

He looks like a tennis god.

Cream-colored shorts, a matching tennis shirt. White tennis shoes that glisten, pure white socks. Blonde hair, a handsome film-star face. He calls out Good Morning, turns to grip the hand of a woman in pink.

Pink tennis dress and matching pink shoes. Black hair nestling under a pink tennis hat.

The door on the street-side opens and a third player emerges. Tall and skinny, a horse-face, wearing Levi cut-offs and a tie-dyed T-shirt.

The woman in pink introduces herself—Teddy Something—and then she introduces the Golden Boy in his tennis whites. His name is Player GL. Seeded in the Tri-State Open, which starts on Friday. The woman's playing mixed doubles. She expects the Golden Boy to win men's singles and men's doubles.

The driver arrives with a folding chair.

After a quick celebrity handshake, and a victory smile, Player GL works out with Levi Cut-Offs. Teddy Something—the woman in pink—watches from her folding chair.

Lester and his pal are awestruck.

Player GL moves like a sleek jungle cat. He gets every ball back. His racket is a golden rapier. His footwork is impeccable. His perfection forces Lester to compare his slash-bang strokes with the golden sweep of Player GL's racket. The comparison makes Lester's tummy go flop-flop.

Player GL took lessons as a little kid.

Ten years ahead of Lester.

There was no way to catch up now.

No way to match his status in the rankings.

No chance of attracting a beautiful, tennis-savvy female with her own limo driver.

But watching Player GL has given Lester a goal: the fluid motion of the backhand slice.

❋ ❋ ❋

Player GL did not win the Tri-State Open tournament that year. The winner was a guy with G.I.-issue eye-glasses and a miraculous, God-given half-volley, picking up every low-lying ball driven at his shoelaces, dink-slicing it low across the net, forcing his opponents to dig for the return. His name was Player JD and he was headed for the Air Force.

Lester marveled at the touch, the control, the on-court poise. James Dye made it look easy. Eyes tracking the ball at his feet. A tennis style that did not demand hitting hard.

Men's doubles came after Men's singles. Four guys in white, controlled hits, twist serves, savvy lobs, drop shots from one guy wearing thick-lensed glasses. He was Player GI from Austin. He hit a spin ball serve and followed it to the net. Lester had never seen anything like it. How could he learn that spin?

※ ※ ※

The last finals match was mixed doubles, where the lady in pink, Teddy Something, won the trophy by partnering with a heavy guy who called himself Colonel something.

She was quite a player.

Colorful. Smart. A take-no-prisoners killer instinct. Missed very few shots. And clever enough to choose a winning partner.

And when Lester congratulated the woman in pink, she confided one of the secrets of winning tennis: "That Colonel, you know—there's a man who keeps the ball low to the ground—making our opponents hit up, just right for the kill-shot putaway from little old me—what's your name, anyway, hon?"

※ ※ ※

Confused, heart-struck and bristling with envy, Lester stood on the sidewalk at Ellwood Park in Amarillo, watching the big black limo turn the corner, Player GL and his entourage, headed for the tennis big-time.

In the next 15 minutes, what remained of the morning work-out, Lester practiced the half-volley of James Dye.

Curious.

It was easy if you kept your eye on the ball.

If you used the Continental grip.

If your footwork worked.

MODESTO JUNIOR COLLEGE

Lester's smarter high school friends went east to college. Yale. Dartmouth. Harvard. MIT. Carnegie Tech.
Three engineer buddies went south to Rice University in Houston.
The playboy party-guys from high school followed the high school party girls—they motored north to Oklahoma.
A gaggle of very smart brainy girls from Lester's neighborhood headed south to Austin, to work the machinery of Grecian mate selection—sororities and fraternities—at the University of Texas, where the male-female ratio was a fabulous 7-2, where girls latched onto guys grinding their way through law school or engineering—plotting a course that led to a monster picket-fence mansion in Houston's River Oaks or Highland Park in Dallas.
Silly stuff.

❈ ❈ ❈

Lester headed west to California, where a tennis friend, Donny S., had moved with his family. The family offered Lester room and board. Great food, a soft bed, trimming the number of unknowns—his first year away from home. .
Donny's Uncle Bill taught English at Modesto Junior College,

which also was the tennis home of Coach FE a fellow lefty, rated number three in college tennis coaches, and Lester's first real tennis coach.

As an old man looking back, Lester held tight onto five memories from Modesto:

Memory One: 10 lessons from Coach FE.

Memory Two: getting to play a match against a future Davis Cupper, a dude from Mexico.

Memory Three: Davis Cup vs. The Air Force—Player PC meets his match in the California desert.

Memory Four: Rosewall, Kramer—the pro tour comes to San Jose. Memory Five: catching a lifelong case of the jock-itch.

* * *

Memory One: 10 Lessons from Coach FE.

Coach FE was a fellow lefty. He owned the first Swoosh forehand Lester had seen up close. To fix his grip problem—and his vast ignorance of the game—Lester signed up for ten private lessons with Coach FE. Five dollars an hour, the weight of coaching wisdom heavy on Lester's amateurish beginner shoulders, swinging away on Saturday mornings, wondering if he would ever get it.

At eighteen, Lester lacked the savvy to ask Coach FE how he had gotten his Swoosh forehand.

Did it start from birth?

A good coach when he was a kid?

A picture in a book?

A lucky set of tennis genes?

The Coach's forehand was natural, effortless, automatic, deadly.

Short backswing.

Slight torso turn.

Strings contact the ball and the ball shoots off the string-

bed and it happens in a split-second.
Catching Lester unawares.
Lester saw the ball coming at him
Medium pace, turning in the air, no sweat.
But way faster than it looked.
Forcing a late return from Lester.
Another feed.
Another late return.
Lester was panting now, moving, holding his breath.
Two backhands, one forehand.
The ball from Coach Earl was relentless.
Looking back at those lessons with the hindsight of old age, Lester saw that Coach Earl had the same Swoosh Forehand motion owned by Coach MB.
But on the left-hand side.
That forehand divided the world of tennis.
If you had the Swoosh, you were a winner.
If you did not have the Swoosh, you were a loser.
The Modesto tennis team had 12 guys.
Lester was player number 12—and he felt like number 13—lucky to be included.

※ ※ ※

Memory Two: Playing a tennis match against a future Davis Cupper.
Lester's learning curve got steeper on a Saturday morning on a tennis court in the town of Lido, 40 miles north of Modesto, where he played a first-round match against Player PC, the number one player on the Modesto team.
From Modesto, Pancho went on to USC, where he won the NCAA doubles with Player JR, the number two player at Modesto. In 1956, Pancho won the NCAA championships again, partnering with tennis great, Alex Olmedo.
When he returned to Mexico, Pancho played Davis Cup

doubles. Later in life, he captained the Mexican Davis Cup team.

And this was the guy across the net from Lester, who had signed up on the advice of Coach Earl—because Lester needed tournament experience.

Could he make it through a whole match?

Lester didn't want to set foot on the same court with Pancho.

But there was the Coach, right beside him.

Show him your best, Flash.

During the short warm-up, Lester kept smiling.

His arm was frozen. His feet had forgotten the tennis footwork practiced in the lessons with the Coach.

When Pancho won the toss and elected to receive, Lester chose the sunny side. Get the ball in play. Show this Pancho guy something.

But Lester's serves could not find the court.

He hit long. He hit wide. He hit the net. He felt absurd. Nerves.

Pancho's racket was a magic wand.

The service ball looked slow and easy coming at Lester, who, in his manic hyper-ventilated confusion, saw the ball rotating in the soft California air. His brain said spin. His body did not react. Not enough experience. Not enough drills. Not enough coaching.

Then the ball touched down and jumped to one side, chest high, right to Lester's back-hand—turning in the air, going crazy when it hit.

Surprised, Lester swung and caught the ball at the last possible second.

A frame-shot, bringing a murmur from the crowd.

Lester's return flopped over the net where Pancho was waiting. He ended the point with a soft placement to the corner.

Nightmare tennis in the California sun.

Lester lost to Pancho, who went on to win the Lodi tournament.

They shook hands at the net and Pancho tried to make

Lester feel better.

Good match, my amigo. You played well.

Thanks, Pancho. You're the greatest.

The lesson: Lester's loss on that hometown Lodi tennis court set him up for a lifetime of learning the game of tennis. He was too late for childhood lessons. But not too late to learn about the game. He would never know everything—he would never play the big-time. He was stuck with his DNA.

He was slow.

He was late getting to the ball.

His tactics, born of panic, were amateurish.

With the right help, he could fix the tactics problem.

That Sunday morning when Lester lost at Lodi, he had been 18 and Pancho had been 19. But Lester was a boy and Pancho was a man—whose tennis savvy put him on a level with the pros.

But the lesson for Lester —one that he never forgot—was permission to hit every ball with maximum spin.

* * *

Memory Three: the subtle, quasi-invisible fabric of the tennis world.

Two weeks after Lester's loss to Player PC, Coal Earl piled the team into panel trucks. Bring your headgear, the Coach said. And a water bottle.

Two college vans trucked the Modesto College team into the desert, where they met up with a team from Castle Air Force Base. The number one player for the Air Force was James Dye, who, a few months ago, had won the singles trophy at the Tri-State Open in Amarillo.

Lester wanted to say hello, Mr. JD—I saw you play in Amarillo at the Tri-State Open and wow, were you great!

But after Lester and his partner lost in doubles to two nameless unknown air force guys, Lester watched in awe as James Dye tied Player PC in the California desert.

It was the age of wooden rackets. A decade before the Prince oversize and the Fortissimo Bentley, made in Italy. Three decades before the Titanium and Boron.

And both these guys were slow-ballers.

It was a match to remember.

A battle of wits and guile and precision, slow-motion tennis.

Pancho used the Dunlop Maxply, the same racket used by Rod Laver.

James Dye, who used a Slazenger, hit a spin ball—slice, side-spin, sometimes topspin—and then followed the ball to the net. Player PC hit passing shots that looked slow (reported as super-slow from Lester's team-mates watching from the sidelines), slow and teasing, both players using the whole court to work each other and make an opening for a winner.

The two players competed in heroic silence.

They were equally matched.

They split sets. The sun hovered low in the west. Time to get the college boys back to the campus. The two players shook hands. They wished each other luck. Pancho went back to school. James Dye went back to his job in the Air Force.

Back in the college van, heading home to Modesto, Lester told his buddies about watching James Dye win the Tri-State Open tournament in Amarillo. He stressed Dye's grace of movement—as if he was gliding, floating, poised.

They were not impressed.

James Dye needed more power, they said.

Tennis was a power game.

And they were right—without knowing it, they were talking about the future of tennis, which would change when the rackets changed from wood to metal, and then from metal to Boron-Titanium.

But what Lester saw on the court in the California desert was two grown men expressing beauty.

❊ ❊ ❊

Memory Four: Rosewall, Kramer, San Jose.

On a chilly night in a foggy Modesto Winter, Coach Earl drove north to San Jose, taking Lester and his buddy DS and the three Mexican guys to see the Jack Kramer tour in a gymnasium at San Jose State. The players were Aussies and one American, Jack Kramer. Driving up from Modesto, Coach Earl told the guys to watch Rosewall's footwork..

Jack Kramer ran the show, preparing for his role—as tennis grew—to become the Czar of Tennis in America.

The tennis took place on a canvas tarpaulin laid on the wooden gym floor, made tight with slender rope threaded through grommets, running to hooks screwed into the walls at floor level.

Lester sat mesmerized, watching these pros deal with the ball. The ease, the lack of effort, the perfection—they seldom missed a shot. Lester had come to see Ken Rosewall.

Lester counted the steps Rosewall took to hit one ball.

27 steps on a crosscourt forehand.

25 steps on a down-the-line backhand.

The steps were tiny, microscopic, balletic.

The steps were automatic—and Rosewall did the same dance for every single shot.

Watching Rosewall, Lester understood why not just anyone could become a tennis professional.

The pros played exhibition tennis. Some clowning around, some laughs, some standing jokes that outsiders could not understand.

The highlight of the evening for the local crowd was the arrival on court of the local pro. Maybe it was the San Jose coach. Maybe it was the pro at the country club. The guy was in his forties. He wore white, his legs had a winter tan.

The local guy had good strokes, but he lacked the cool finesse of the pro timing. They outfoxed him through some doubles games. Then, as he received serve from the ad-court, the local pro boomed a forehand that was a clean winner. Applause from the crowd. Blushes from the local guy. Thumbs up from the pros.

They were not here to embarrass the local talent.

Before the team hit the road back to Modesto, Coach FE shook hands with Jack Kramer. Then he introduced Player PC and Player JR and Player YM. Up close, Kramer was lean, confident, sharp eyes with a wolfish look.

The three Mexican guys were chatting with Kramer when Coach Earl asked Ken Rosewall what he did to hit a down-the-line backhand loaded with slice.

And keep it inside the lines.

A long moment. Rosewall asked for a quarter. Lester dug in his pocket, held out the coin. Rosewall held the quarter between his thumb and forefinger.

The net is highest there, he said. Thirty-six inches vs. thirty in the middle. If the ball crosses the net any higher than this quarter, then this down-the-line ball would go long.

So much for Lester's dream of becoming a touring tennis pro.

Footnote on sports metaphors:

In his essay on Roger Federer—"Federer Both Flesh and Not"—David Foster Wallace analyzes the metaphors used to describe sports:

"In men's sports no one ever talks about beauty, or grace, or the body. Men may profess their 'love' of sports, but that love must always be cast and enacted in the symbology of war: elimination vs. advance, hierarchy of rank and standing, obsessive stats and technical analysis, tribal and/or nationalist fervor, uniforms, mass noise, banners, chest-thumping, face-painting, etc. For reasons that are not well understood, war's codes are safer for most of us than love's. You too may find them so, in which case Spain's mesomorphic and totally martial Rafael Nadal is the man's man for you—he of the unsleeved biceps and Kabuki self-exhortations."

Metaphors of beauty vs. metaphors of war.

Was there a place for Lester in the brave new tennis world that hovered on the horizon? Was there any way to import the backhand gene from Ken Rosewall?

* * *

Memory Five: the Modesto JC jock-itch.

The jock itch (medical name: tinea cruris) is called the jock-itch because it finds a home in the moisty crotches of male athletes. You get this red rash. The red rash itches. The place of the itch is your groin.

That same 13th place on the tennis team also forced Lester into a line of half-naked guys on a warm autumn afternoon inside the Field House shuffling toward a so-called doctor, a bona fide MD who should have known better, a bored gray-haired part-time college MD standing at a metal table who failed to wash his hands before he took a good grip on Lester's privates, passing to Lester whatever malady swarmed on the privates of the guys who had been ahead in the line.

The doc's hands were not getting sanitized between feels.

Lester was pissed off.

His uncle back in Amarillo was a doctor.

His granddad back in Amarillo was a doctor.

They washed their hands between patients all day long.

But not this guy.

Lester submitted when he should have objected.

He was being polite.

He was respecting his elders.

He feared the ire of the Coach.

The line shuffled forward, pushing Lester along.

No one was talking.

No one but Lester was worried that this idiot doctor was passing unknown germs from one crotch to another.

Three guys away.

Cough for me, the doctor said.

Two guys away.

Cough for me, the doctor said.

One guy away and then Lester —his interior boy-man alarm screaming Do Something, Idiot from Texas!

Cough for me, the doctor said.

Lester did not remember coughing.

He remembered being pissed off.

He remembered looking at the Coach, who watched with his big tennis forearms crossed.

Do something!

He remembered not saying anything.

Six days after the fake pro-forma physical exam, Lester felt the itch in his crotch. Decades later, after trying a dozen different treatments, he still had the itch. Fond memories from Modesto.

THE LONG TENNIS SHADOW OF MODESTO JC

After spending his freshman year at Modesto, Lester joined the great herd of Texas kids at the University of Texas in Austin, where PE (Physical Ed.) was required. When the Coaches at the registration desk saw that Lester had spent a year at Modesto, they made him a deal. If he would teach basic tennis stuff to beginners—strokes, footwork, scoring—they would count that as his PE requirement.

Lester was thrilled.

Modesto JC had a long reach.

But after a year in the Modesto sun, a year of learning from his mistakes, Lester still didn't know the best way to teach the basics of tennis.

He adjusted grips.

He demonstrated strokes.

He used his right hand—most beginners were right-handed.

He felt like an idiot, trying to teach a sport he loved but did not understand.

And then, at mid-term, Lester got a call to try out for the Tennis Team.

Proving once again the long reach of Modesto JC.

✳ ✳ ✳

The Coach at UT-Austin was Wilmer Allison, who had beaten Fred Perry to win the U.S. Championships in 1935, and who had been runner-up to Bill Tilden at Wimbledon in 1930.

Allison's fame was a drawing card for top players.

On Lester's first day at the practice courts, he said hello to an old guy in a straw hat and a three-piece suit. The old guy shook hands with Lester, welcomed him to the team, and pointed him to the court, where three hotshots in all-white were hitting.

The old guy was Dr. Daniel Penick, the father of Texas tennis. An immigrant from the deep south, Dr. Penick ranked second in his class of 1891 at the University of Texas.

In 1900, he started his long-time career at UT-Austin, teaching Greek and Latin. In 1901, he became the unofficial tennis coach.

Looking out onto the courts, Lester felt his knees tremble. His stomach curled itself into a knot. While he sat beside tennis history, observing real tennis in the present tense—

Lester was heart-attack nervous.

Because one of the three guys on the court was Sammy Giammalva, who had big wins over the big tennis names of his day—Vic Seixas, Gustavo Palafox, Barry McKay, Donald Dell.

Lester tripped as he stepped onto the court.

His feet felt heavy—concrete blocks.

Across the net from Sammy G., Lester managed to return one forehand. The re-return from Sammy G. came back fast, a ball shot from a cannon.

Hitting with Sammy G hurt Lester's arm.

Where did the power come from?

Lester had only one insight—Sammy G. possessed a Swoosh forehand that sent the ball zooming at Lester, shot from a howitzer.

One forehand was all it took.

Lester was a slow learner, but that day he learned fast.

He did not belong here, on this sacred Texas tennis turf, facing a major champion with a cannonball swoosh forehand. It reminded him of his match with superior footwork and a world-class presence—like Player PC, back in Lodi.

※ ※ ※

Lester spent the rest of the term rallying with lesser players.

He dropped his desire to dive into the world of tennis. He got smarter about making grades. In college, if you were headed to graduate school, B's were no good. Only A's counted. He made a B in Spanish because all the A's got sucked up by kids from the border—Del Rio, Eagle Pass, Laredo, McAllen, Candelaria—native speakers whose musically trilled R's decimated the Bell Curve.

One of Lester's tennis buddies suggested a Russian class—no competition except for the Mad Greek, an older guy, spending his 11th year on campus, whose native tongue was the source of the Russian alphabet. Lester had a good ear for offbeat languages—he made straight A's in Russian—and an empire-building geography professor recruited him for East European Studies, which had course requirements in Russian History and Russian economics, which was about oil—Russia was the big supplier for Europe.

The papers Lester wrote for East European Studies took him away from *War and Peace* (the novel by Tolstoy) into the global intricacies of supply and demand on the icy steppes—and his papers on Eastern Europe hauled in more A's, paving the pathway to graduate school.

In graduate school—Lester was going for a Ph.D. in English—he invited young East Coast junior hotshot professors in the English Department to play doubles—made them look good, they said hello in the hallway. He saw his grades improve. The grades helped Lester propose marriage—his chosen wife-to-be was a brainy Pi Phi who graduated with a double major in religion and philosophy—she thought Lester was funny.

* * *

In Austin, Lester played with a membership at the Caswell Tennis Center. His first time on orange Texas clay, white chalk lines, funny bounces. His last year in grad school, he was sitting in the bleachers when he was recruited by Player GI to play singles.

Player GI from the Tri-State Open, Amarillo, Ellwood Park, almost a decade ago.

Player GI with the twisted barbed-hook serve and the immaculate backhand slice.

Player GI with the thick eyeglasses.

They played a set. Lester won. He was overwhelmed with wonder. Friends of Player GI got recruited for doubles and Lester froze and Player GI—who had coached tennis—said: "Step into that forehand. Hit the ball like you mean it. Don't let these people win."

Lester followed orders. He stepped in. His shots got better. The tennis court was a magic rectangle. For one long moment, Lester was the magician.

* * *

With the Ph.D. a sure-thing, Lester entrained for Chicago, the annual meeting of the Modern Language Association, where he interviewed for a job at the MLA and wound up at Beloit College in Wisconsin, land of endless winters, where he played indoor tennis at Rockford, 20 miles to the south, on the ice-rimmed edge of northern Illinois, driving through snow and sleet to play chilly tennis in a building with low ceilings and drafty courts—hardly a tennis cathedral—which fired up Lester's plan to elude the bitter winter and head back to

California.

Modesto—hear me calling!

His memorable match in the frozen kingdom of ice and snow was played against a visiting poet, Galway Kinnell—a net rusher who played with poetic abandon, who took two sets and allowed Lester one—and penned a serious tennis poem—perhaps inspired by his match with Lester on the green floor of the indoor tennis center in Rockford, Illinois—here's an excerpt—

> among the pure
> right angles and unhesitating lines
> of this arena where every man grows old
> pursuing that repertoire of perfect shots,
> darkness already in his strokes,
> even in death cramps squeezing a tennis ball
> for arm strength, to the disgust of the night nurse,
> and smiling; and a few hours later found dead
> –
> the smile still in place but the ice bag
> left cooling the brow now mysteriously
> icing the right elbow....

Darkness in his strokes?
Every man grows old?
Time to head west.

ESCAPE TO CALIFORNIA

It took Lester a decade of wintry survival-tactics before he found an escape from the icy Wisconsin winters. Escape came through his wife, Mrs. Lester, who had a brother in San Diego, where it did not snow in the winter.

The timing was good.

Lester's college was in the middle of the New Plan—three terms, fall-winter-summer, the school stayed open all year. In a four-year period, a total of twelve terms, students would be on campus for eight terms—of their own design. Faculty could choose when to teach. Lester could teach Summer and Fall, and escape the midwestern winter.

Lester's lust to escape the ice and snow so was powerful that he did not suspect Mrs. Lester's secret plan, triggered by Edgar Cayce, the Sleeping Profit, who worked the edges of the New Age by sleeping. On coming awake, Edgar would announce the hot new notion, a product of his profoundest sleep. Mrs. Lester's plan would unveil itself when the I-Ching hexagram was ready to transmit.

The Lesters found a rental at the Point Loma Tennis Club in San Diego. Mrs. Lester joined a women's group that studied Edgar Cayce—and got more proficient with the I-Ching. Lester took lessons from the pro, a hippy Brit with wild hair, who had tried his luck on the circuit, and was now stuck in San Diego. The pro was one of the many targets of Bobby Riggs, a gambler who played for money.

Lester was a tennis history hound. Riggs was the world number 1 amateur in 1939, the year he won men's singles, men's doubles, and mixed doubles at Wimbledon. Decades later, Riggs would show up at the PLTC to bait the British pro into playing doubles for money. Riggs would beat the pro by mixing stratospheric lobs with taunting remarks. No one knew that Riggs was training for his match against Billie Jean King, immortalized on TV as The Battle of the Sexes, in 1973.

* * *

Life in San Diego was easy. Light traffic. Great weather. Easy shopping on Point Loma. And it took Lester only three weeks to find his own A-Team.

About time.

First, he got shut out, the age-old story of excluding the unknown.

On his first Sunday at the PLTC, Lester suited up. His legs were winter-pale. His white shorts felt one size too small—they hadn't been worn since October. But he was here in California, saved from the ice. The sun was out. The tennis courts were right outside his rented condo. He couldn't help not knowing any tennis players. He didn't relish begging to be let into a foursome.

Maybe he could find a pickup game.

Three people who needed a fourth.

It was cool in the morning shade.

Lester shivered.

Then he edged himself into the sun. That felt good. The California warmth boded good luck on its way. All four courts were full. On Court One, the star of the club—his name was Kent —was playing mixed doubles.

Kent's partner was slim and attractive.

A California blonde.

Their opponents—both in white—were not so slim and attractive—but they moved like they owned the court.

Kent was tall, lean, tanned and California suave. Women would give him big smiles. He moved with movie-esque precision. His strokes were tennis photo perfect, smooth easy backswing, solid contact with the ball, a photo finish follow-through—another lucky recipient of those early childhood lessons.

After a set, Kent's male opponent hurried off the court, leaving Kent alone with the two women.

Lester stood up.

Made himself visible.

He didn't call out—he was a quiet boxed-in guy with a Ph.D.

But his stance telegraphed that he was ready to play. Eager to be invited.

But would he get invited?

Kent glanced over, then looked away.

One of the women glanced over.

She turned her back to Lester.

He was the Outsider.

He sat back down. He watched as the threesome played Australian, two on one.

Lester felt the sadness of being excluded.

❋ ❋ ❋

His first move on Monday was to book time with the pro—whose main teaching technique was shouting at Lester to move faster.

Run, Lester!

You're too lazy, Lester!

Show me you care!

After the lesson, the Hippy Pro invited Lester to play doubles. He missed a ton of shots. Playing outdoors was not like playing indoors. The sun kept getting in his eyes. He needed a better sun-hat. He needed tinted lenses. He booked another lesson with the pro.

At the Friday cocktail social, the Hippy Pro introduced Lester to Player BC, a handsome tanned guy with a wacko sense of humor, who grabbed Lester as a fourth for Saturday morning. The other players were Bert and Ron. Lester, honing his lob and drop-shot and half-volley skills, fit right in. The teams split sets. They made a date to play again.

Lester felt right at home at the PLTC.

He had found his own A-Team.

Playing outdoors in the San Diego sun gave Lester a slight tan. His wife commented on how relaxed he looked. She was busy with her women's group—she talked about getting a second car.

Lester's doubles group lacked the magical precision of the original Four Musketeers (boys 12 years old) from his Texas childhood, while Lester watched from a distance in the November wind outside Wolflin School, but there was enough solidarity among the four buddies to pay debonair Kent back on the next Sunday when he arrived at the courts looking for a game, presenting himself at courtside, flexing his muscles, brushing back a stray lock of hair, looking with expectation at Lester's foursome.

And when Bert had to leave early, Lester and his buds played Australian.

Leaving handsome Kent on the sidelines.

Thinking back on his behavior, Lester felt silly.

His need for vengeance had swept aside his intelligence—his threesome could have used a fourth. Maybe his tennis buddies didn't like handsome Kent, either.

But Lester relished being A-Team at last.

SO LONG ICE, GOODBYE SNOW

When the San Diego spring edged toward summer, the Lesters drove back to the Midwest—he owed the college two terms, payment for his winter in paradise. Their house was intact. Lester took the death-dive back into teaching and got trapped by faculty committee meetings. Through the Edgar Cayce study group, his wife made a connection with a Buddhist scholar in Sausalito. After reading two of his books, Mrs. Lester remarked that this Buddhist scholar needed an editor.

They did the dishes together. Lester went upstairs to his study. He marked student papers. He wrote four tentative pages on his new book—Murder on Court One—starring a bitter battered tennis pro who had taken a job at a fancy Texas tennis club after he was forced off the circuit by his aging knees.

The summer flew by.

Playing with the college basketball coach as his partner, Lester got to the semi-finals in doubles in a local tennis tournament. The Coach remarked on the improvement of Lester's game. Summer ended with a rainstorm. Autumn leaves buried Lester's yard. Snow fell on Halloween. Mrs. Lester had a minor accident when her tires slid on the ice. Lester checked the calendar, counting the days until they could get back to San Diego.

He and his wife talked about buying the corner condo. She told him to go ahead. Why was she being so understanding? The down payment was small. The monthly payments were doable.

* * *

On the phone with the manager at the PLTC, Lester bought the corner condo. A wave of relief blew through him. On the scoreboard inside his head, he saw four words: Escape the Falling Snow.

At the end of December, Lester and his wife turned the house keys over to their renter, a new faculty member in the music department, and headed to California. On their first night away from home, their car got snowed in. On the second day, their car hit a patch of ice. Mrs. Lester screamed as Lester slammed the gearshift into Low. Their car did a single spin, then slid off the road, crunched to a stop. A trucker used a chain to pull Lester back onto the highway. Lester tipped the guy ten bucks.

They had plotted a westward route out of the Midwest, through Colorado. With the almost-accident, Lester turned south, heading for the sun. This route would take a day longer. Amarillo, Albuquerque, Kingman, San Diego.

Safe in their condo at the PLTC, they watched the weather news.

Snow.

Ice.

Wind.

Midwest nightmare madness.

While Lester played doubles, his wife redecorated their condo. She got advice from her Edgar Casey friends. She started writing a book about the after-life as filtered through Edgar Cayce.

She kept in touch with the guru in Sausalito.

* * *

The hippy tennis pro was gone. The PLTC was under new management. Lester volunteered for the tennis committee. The other members wanted to run a tennis clinic for the residents. Lester had been reading tennis books. He made some suggestions. The head of the committee said Welcome Back, Lester.

He felt more at home.

The tennis clinic gave Lester some feedback on his life.

He was not bad as a tennis instructor.

He got the players tossing the tennis ball, watching for the spin.

He adjusted a couple of grips.

He remembered stuff from his tennis books—winter reading.

The time whizzed by. Lester and the first Mrs. Lester joined the PLTC book club. She was a careful reader. She had majored in philosophy and religion, but she had a Ph.D. in English, with a focus on the romantic poets. She wound up taking charge of the book club discussion. Lester was impressed. He was not so impressed the next week, when Mrs. L said she had a job offer to edit the writings of this mysterious Buddhist guru—a job offer that would whisk her all the way to a hippie commune in the mountains outside Sausalito.

Why did he pick you? Lester said.

Buddhism, she said.

Any connection to Old Edgar C?

I wish you wouldn't make fun, Lester.

Sorry.

Also, I'm certain that he's a bodhisattva.

What's he paying you?

Room and board and a stipend when the book gets published.

How long are you going for?

I'll see you at home, she said.

I might not be at home, he said.

Well, then, I'll see you wherever.

So we're still on schedule with your life turning a corner every seven years?

You're safe here, Lester. You're right at home. You've got your own A-Team. You said you wanted to teach tennis. That crazy pro has vanished.

I need some education, he said. I don't know squat about teaching tennis.

You're a great teacher, she said. Go for it.

PART V

RE-LEARNING THE GAME OF TENNIS

ALL ALONE IN CALIFORNIA

So the I-Ching directed Lester's wife to go north, and she was gone the next week, and Lester's condo echoed with emptiness.

Lester was in shock. He got calls from his in-laws, asking what had happened. The sleeping prophet, Lester said. He told her to go.

Lester's reply put his in-laws in shock.

He felt lonely. He looked at women and wondered how he could connect. Pretty faces. Sweet smiles. His heart felt broken. He got invited to play mixed doubles. A woman with a condo near the pool asked him to a party. He had trouble talking to other women. He played too much tennis. He hurt his knee, his first real injury—that kept him off the court for six weeks.

He could not be getting old.

He wasn't fifty yet.

He found help: a doctor, a chiropractor, a homeopath, a dentist. He was due back at Beloit. He called the Dean who called the chairman and got a leave of absence—if Lester agreed to teach four terms in a row—sixteen endless months in the frozen mortuary of the Midwest.

* * *

He taught his first tennis lesson to a teenage girl with a bad leg. Her mother wrote him a check for five dollars—his first money as a tennis teacher. He worked on his tennis novel. An agent in L.A. was interested. Lester found a writer's group. The critiques were tough. He met a poet who was beautiful and twenty years younger. After an awkward dinner date, she advised him to find someone his own age. Was he that old already? A realtor from back home in the Midwest called about renting Lester's house, two blocks from the college. The rent would make the condo payment, with money left over.

Lester teetered on the brink of a new life.

He needed some training.

In his tennis teaching, Lester was waiting for the student who was savvy enough to want a slice backhand, in homage to Player GL, the Golden Boy from the Midwest. One student was not enough. He needed more students. He knew how to teach writing and literature—but he didn't know how to teach a tennis class. Where could Lester study the art of teaching tennis?

A tennis friend told Lester about a 10-day seminar, on the courts at the University of Redlands, in the desert east of Los Angeles. He wrote to his wife.

She wrote him back: go for it.

The head honcho would change Lester's life. His name was Dennis Van Der Meer.

TENNIS WITH DENNIS

Dennis Van Der Meer entered the room. He was six-feet, lean, tanned legs, a healthy head of curly blond hair, a good smile, sharp blue eyes, and a brain for detail. Thirty students in the room, they introduced themselves—there were three Bills—and when the last person gave her name, Dennis went around the room, person to person to person, calling each name, without a list on a clipboard.

Lester was impressed. As a college-level teacher, he knew the importance of the first seven minutes. This Van Der Meer guy was a wizard.

The first group exercise was a lesson on the serve, the single most important shot in tennis. Not a serving lesson on the courts—workable hard courts connected to the University, lighted for evening play in the quick desert cold—but a lesson in hitting up on the ball.

Follow me, Dennis said.

He led the students through the back gate, away from the courts, into the brambles on the ugly side of the chain link fence that separated the courts from the desert dirt.

There were murmurs as thirty students followed Van Der Meer out the narrow gate, onto the dry sandy dirt rife with cacti and thorns and the sharp rocks of the California desert.

Hit your normal serve, Dennis said. When you clear the

fence three times from outside the courts, join the rest of us inside.

Lester was impressed with Van Der Meer's strategy. The tennis net was 36 inches high at the posts, 30 inches high at the center strap. A lot of serves hit the net, 30 inches on the strap in the middle, because the servers did not hit up on he serve—they hit down. From outside the court, the word "net" reduced itself to a metaphor—the real net was the fence, ten feet tall. Ten feet is 120 inches. The group serves had to clear a small mountain top.

As the grumbles started, service motions cranked up and balls slapped the fence on the outside. Anyone with a crappy service motion would be hitting straight and flat, with no arc, and this exercise would reveal, in the first minutes, who needed work on their serve.

And who might spend half an hour outside the fence.

※ ※ ※

This was brilliant teaching. Show and don't tell. Right from the start, Dennis made his people think about the serve and its trajectory. To hit a serve over the net, you have to get your strings under the ball. Even if you were tall, and used to hitting down from your height, serving at the fence made you hit up.

At the same time, Lester was slow to take action. He was miffed. He had a good serve—the legacy of chopping wood as a teenager at a summer cabin in New Mexico—but his first few serves caromed off the fence. So he went into exaggeration—hitting way higher than he thought he needed to—and Voila! the ball cleared the fence, a small cheer went up, and Lester hit three more, just to make sure that it was no accident, and then headed inside.

Lester was amused, he was impressed. The fence was Lester's friend. He had never thought about hitting up on the serve.

Back on the courts—no dust, no sand, no desert bugs,

no burrs or stickers—the group was united. They lined up standing in the alley—fifteen and fifteen—while Van Der Meer demonstrated the slow-motion serve—breaking it down into six parts:

1. Balanced stance.
2. Ball Toss.
3. Racquet drop.
4. Back-scratch.
5. Contact.
6. Follow-through

Without using a ball, Lester and his fellow-students practiced the slow-motion serve. Lots of grumbling from the real jocks, but Lester loved the idea. Simple. Obvious. Thoughtful. Useful for teaching beginners. Useful for veterans with crappy serves.

Practice it indoors, Van Der Meer said. In front of a mirror.

❊ ❊ ❊

Before he sent them off, Van Der Meer told four hitters to rally in the short court—a great teaching tool. The rally ball had to clear the net. Then it needed to drop down into the service court. Four people. Start with hitting down the line. Then switch to cross-court.

This single exercise helped Lester's control, forcing him to hit soft. Forced his feet to be more precise setting up. Forced him to use topspin. Which forced him to change grips, from the Continental to the Eastern. Another great teaching tool. Good for kids, who needed control. And good for seniors, warming up in the short court.

While the students rallied, sweating in the cool desert air, Dennis walked around, observing his students stumbling, trapped in the service box, trying to hit soft when all their lives they had tried to hit hard. A blonde woman in a track suit jotted down his notes on a clipboard. That blonde in the track suit with her little clipboard—was she an archetypal fixture in tennis schools? She had many roles—Secretary, help-meet, happy smiling advertisement. Maybe if Lester started his own tennis school, she would appear, a genie from a can of tennis balls, smiling, capable, perfect hair, wearing a track suit, hugging her clipboard, ready to jot down the wisdom spouted from Lester San Marino, the Guru of Tennis.

Those notes Van Der Meer dictated on that first chilly desert evening would turn up on the tenth day, at the end of the ten-day workshop: "With a little work, Lester can be a solid B club player."

Van Der Meer's signature stroke was the forehand. The next morning he started off with a demo—the ready position for the torso and both hands. Racquet head up, left hand on the throat, the shoulders turned one-quarter. He wanted the torso turned, the eyes on the oncoming ball. He called it the quarter-turn. It didn't seem like much, but the minute he followed instructions and tried the quarter-turn, Lester's forehand got better. He was ready. He was alert. He was on the ball.

* * *

As the week progressed, Lester learned a lot. He met people. He formed his own A-Team. And he kept waiting for the break-through tips on the backhand—the same precision, the same quarter-turn.

The backhand break-through never happened. They did volleys. They did half-volleys. They got a demo of pronation, using a push-broom for emphasis. But Van Der Meer had not worked out the same simple solution for the backhand. So that left a big hole in his teaching technique, proving he was human, just a little. And in recreational social tennis—mimicking the pros—the forehand was the big shot. Looking back on that ten-day session, Lester saw how lucky he was, taking the court every morning, in winter, under a soft California sun. Hearing, from the other courts, the patter of tennis shoes getting their owners into position.

As he drove back to San Diego, Lester was eager to do some teaching. He wanted to see what worked with beginners. His tennis-teaching self was heating up.

❋ ❋ ❋

(Aside: Two years after that first Van Der Meer training camp, Lester went back to Redlands for a refresher course run by Coach Jim Verdieck, who had assisted Van Der Meer in the ten-day workshop, and who had called Lester "Glasses." And when it came time to demonstrate the half-volley he called Lester out —"Hey Glasses, come on down."—and Lester's timing was on that day, and he loved basking in the metaphorical spot-light, his moment onstage. It was winter in California, just the right medium temperature for his red and blue tennis outfit, and his feet borrowed their performance from Rosewall and his racket arm was steady (just like Rod Laver) and his knees bent without any amateur fuss, lowering his center of gravity down to the ball —and the half-volley had always been easy for Lester, because he didn't have to run, all he had to do was keep his eyes down, get set, and let the racket do the work. When the demo was done, when he had received the high-sign from Coach Verdieck, Lester wished he could do it all over again. He liked not missing. He liked being watched. He liked feeling like a real tennis pro. Thank you, Dennis. Thank you, Coach Verdieck.)

WITH A SMIDGEN OF TENNIS EDUCATION LESTER LANDS A TENNIS JOB

Back home in San Diego, Lester interviewed for a job heading the tennis program at the University Village tennis complex. In his interview, he used his Van Der Meer learning to demonstrate the proper grip for the backhand slice. Ten days with Dennis and Lester was way ahead in his group-teaching.

He got the job.
He worked three nights a week.
He took a woman to dinner.
He spoke to his wife on the phone. She was having a friend back home send clothes to Sausalito. Lester phoned the Dean of his Midwest college. He wanted to resign. The Dean checked with the chairman, who wrote to Lester: "You are irreplaceable, Lester, but not indispensable."

Lester had medical coverage until the end of Spring. He used the medical coverage to pay for a doctor for his first tennis injury, a twisted knee. He used a cane. He wore his first knee brace.

Women from his group lesson asked about his knee. Their voices sounded different. Interested, with a hint of promise.

He took another woman to dinner. The conversation was not memorable, the woman had no sense of humor.

Lester had thrived in academia for two decades. In that cozy ivy-walled world, the women were educated, they read books. Outside the walls of academe, the women were quick and cute and bright-eyed. They took tennis lessons to keep the weight off. Lester was learning about life outside academe.

But with more tennis work, Lester needed more tennis education. He signed up for a long weekend with Vic Braden.

HITTING LANES AT THE VIC BRADEN TENNIS COLLEGE

Lester's second intensive tennis learning experience was the Vic Braden Tennis College at Coto de Caza, California, near Mission Viejo, three days side-by-side with a covey of tennis coaches aching for tennis fame.

Vic Braden was medium height, a round happy face, a master-salesman's delivery, selling his stroke production system. Where Van Der Meer had haunted the courts, stepping in to demonstrate the forehand ready-position, the stroke, the follow-through, Vic Braden stood on a stage, backed by diagrams of the Vic Braden Forehand, which looked to Lester like the Van Der Meer forehand, but with better promo-art. Both systems emphasized the ready position, racket head up, left hand on the throat, shoulders in the quarter turn. Both emphasized the Jack Kramer/Don Budge follow-through—racket on edge, pointing at the far fence behind your opponent. No hints of the windshield wiper follow-through made possible by Boron-Titanium—two decades away.

* * *

The Braden Tennis College was an on-site facility, not a traveling tennis show, a la Van Der Meer. Coto de Caza was a corporate venture, financed by Chevron and major land-developer Arvida Corp., touted as a sanctuary for wildlife, a gate-guarded community with upscale living and safety for the family.

Vic like to lecture—his specialty was the forehand. He was funny, lots of tennis asides—if a tennis ball collides with your face, that's a fuzz sandwich.

Lester spent time in his favorite hitting lane, working on his backhand volley. There were seventeen hitting lanes, pie-shaped cubicles where you could have balls fed to you—and where the work Lester did perked up his volleys. A real confidence builder.

Vic had cameras stashed on the court, along with water fountains and chilled orange slices. When you finished a workout, you could go into a viewing booth (Vic had four) and check out the mechanics of your serve.

Watching himself on the screen, Lester was happy that his service motion was okay, no major flaws. He detected a caution in his stance, a reluctance to put everything into one shot. In his mid-forties, Lester discovered he was conserving his energy. Energy was finite. He was getting older.

Was he crazy trying to make it in a world dominated by jocks

There were mostly jocks at Vic's place. Jocks with muscles and fine well-honed musculature and sharp athlete's eyes. Tennis jocks who had played well in college. Some of them had been on the "tour," playing the circuit, moving from country to country, testing their games against other jocks, assessing their chances of playing big-time.

These guys were tough competition. Lester never kidded himself—he did not have the muscular equipment, or the visual savvy, to be a jock. Jocks had better timing. They lived by the killer instinct—win or die. Jocks didn't take the court to hit a clean topspin forehand. They took the court to decimate the enemy. To a lot of the jocks at Vic's school, tennis was a blood sport.

* * *

On his last day at Vic's place, Lester was in the hitting lane, working on his volley, rat-tat-tat, feeling perfect that day, when William Shatner of *Star Trek* fame showed up with his kid, who was toting a racket. Sensing the spotlight, Lester demonstrated the Vic Braden volley technique, arm and forearm keeping the racket head high (the Rod Laver technique)—the memory-trigger was making the L-shape, making sure to step forward as you volley, using body weight instead of muscle, the tip of the racket staying level with your eyeball.

When Lester got all that together—arm, wrist, L-shape, eye—his volley was picture-perfect.

Lester headed to the last class with Vic expounding onstage while Shatner took his kid back up the beam, back to the good ship Enterprise. It could only happen in Southern California.

* * *

As Lester drove back to San Diego, he compared his time with Dennis and Vic. Both Braden and Van Der Meer had focused on the forehand. And Lester didn't see much difference. Van Der Meer had been clever with his drills and exercises. Vic Braden had been clever with his emplacements—if Lester ever had a place to plant it, he would install a pie-shaped hitting lane, and charge admission. Van Der Meer walked around the courts, handing out advice, checking to see who was doing the drills. But Vic Braden left the on-court teaching to a covey of tennis jocks, hefty muscular guys edging toward middle age.

Lots of women students.

Only one woman instructor.

The big insights at Van Der Meer's had been the slo-mo

serve and learning from the short-court. The big insight at Vic's place was Lester's volley, sharpened by the pie-shaped hitting lane—a place to work on your volley alone.

Both Van Der Meer and Vic Braden were tennis gurus—big-time salesmen with crowd-pleasing spiels, edging toward pontification—not unlike the Buddhist guru who had used the I-Ching to enchant Mrs. Lester, luring her north to Sausalito.

Feeling pumped with tennis lore, Lester was a better teacher. The money dribbled in. His knee was still hurting and his elbow required a strap. When he had a chance to play doubles, he was sharper. He knew the angles. Women invited him to play mixed doubles. He took them to dinner. But looking at his future, he knew his body would not hold up, mostly because of his non-jock status.

* * *

As an aspiring tennis pro, Lester conjured the cost of doing business as a tennis pro.

Vic Braden had to make a ton of money to keep his campus afloat. Equipment was expensive—the hitting lanes, the video booth—the meeting room where Vic sold his product, and multiple tennis-pro employees. Vic never showed up on a court.

Van Der Meer, on the other hand, spent every day on the court. He leased college courts for ten days. He had two employees.

Would that mean more take-home pay for Dennis?

Did Lester want to travel?

Did he want the headache of owning his own facility?

Lester liked teaching. He liked learning about the game. He was edging into the San Diego tennis community. And there was a pro in Lester's neighborhood who ran a tennis program that employed some very savvy tennis people, so Lester signed up for a weekend with Ed Collins.

IN THE GROOVE WITH ED COLLINS

Lester's third tennis school was with Ed Collins, the founder of the Peninsula Tennis Club in San Diego, not far from the Del Mar Racing Track. When the wind blew, you could smell the horses.

Ed Collins was a shrewd teacher, good with groups, good sense of humor. He was not as famous as Dennis and Vic, but he knew how to handle large groups. His first move on opening night—the schedule was Friday night, Saturday, and Sunday morning—was to slow things down. On a chilly Friday evening, 30 weekend students stood in a ragged formation while Ed demonstrated the service motion.

First he demonstrated at match-speed. The demo was a blur. No way to learn that way. Then he slowed down, breaking the service motion into parts:

1. Balanced stance.
2. Ball Toss.
3. Racquet drop.
4. Back-scratch.
5. Contact.
6. Follow-through.

Then he took the group through the steps, slowing down. Then the group did the whole motion together, thirty rackets slowed down, while Ed walked around, observing.

He walked past Lester, who was in the zone. When Ed reached the end of the line, he came back to Lester. He stood there for half a minute, and Lester felt the heat in his face. Ed Collins called out to the group. He wanted everyone to stop. Lester was on a stage, lit up by a blinding spotlight—he sensed a demerit zooming his way. It was no fun being the first guy in the group to make a boo-boo. Maybe he would be escorted out by armed tennis assistants, beefy jocks, all in white. Then Ed said: "People, look over here, watch this guy Lester. People, we have a genius amongst us!"

Lester blushed. He loved the limelight.

* * *

Then Ed asked Lester to demonstrate his slo-mo serve. Time to remember what he had learned from Van Der Meer. Classmates stood in a silent circle. Lester felt the hot burn of spotlights as he went through the steps of the slow-motion serve, the balanced stance, the slo-mo backswing, the imaginary well-timed ball toss, the back scratch, the arm and wrist coming up, the wrist bending, the imaginary contact when strings met the ball, the slow-mo pronation as the ball leaves the strings, then the follow-through. Lester felt smug. His work with Van Der Meer had paid off. The six-step ritual was so basic and so easy that Lester had used it in his group classes at University City.

He added deep breathing.

And his own serve was more consistent—sharper angles, fewer double-faults.

But fame was always fleeting, and Lester's moment at the weekend clinic lasted until the focus shifted to the service return—and Lester's fame became a thing of the recent past. Would there be another Golden Moment under the aegis of Ed Collins?

* * *

Friday night ended on a happy note—Ed Collins had noticed Lester. Saturday morning went well—People said hello, Lester, how's it going, bud? And then, just before lunch break, Ed's smartly-dressed helpers put the students through a consistency drill—Last Man Standing. Two teams of six hit a single ball back and forth across the net. After you hit, then you jogged to the other baseline, where you had another hit. If you missed, you dropped out. If you made a deliberate kill, you were out. Lester could still run in those days, and he was used to hitting the ball high and deep, for teaching purposes, and for friendly A-Team doubles.

The whole court was his target. Take your time.

Lester's first shot was a lob. His second shot was a lob. The lobs were high and deep, giving him time to jog around the net post, and get set up to return the next ball. He made sure to lob with a follow-through. Hang onto it longer. Lift with your legs. Lob with control.

As the players missed and dropped out, Lester kept moving. He was one against three, then one against two, he lobbed higher, giving himself more time. His lobs hung high in the heavy beach-front California air. People on the sidelines chanted Lester, Lester, Lester.

Another hitter dropped out, leaving just two gladiators—Lester against a heavy guy with huge muscles, fast on his feet, a blood-sport aficionado who was out to beat Lester at this game. An aficionado with a frustrated face. Lester felt like a genius. When Lester was rounding the court for one more hit, Ed Collins asked the group: "What is Lester doing? Is he hitting hard?"

And a squeaky voice said: "Lester's lobbing again!" The heavy set guy lost his patience, tried for a kill, hit too hard and the ball was out. Applause for Lester. This time the fame felt more fleeting.

Lunch was salad and potato chips. Lester needed a nap. He faked his way through the afternoon. He motored home to the PLTC, where his sleep was fast and deep.

Lester didn't know it—but he was feeling his age.

* * *

To cap off the Sunday morning workshop, Ed brought out one of his instructors, a thirty-something red-headed guy with a close-cropped beard and a solid physique that reminded Lester of Carlos Moya, a champion from Spain who later became the Coach of Rafael Nadal. The red beard guy was solid. He was uniform, controlled, effortless, nothing flashy, as he rallied with two other guys who worked for Ed. Tennis was his profession. He did not miss a shot. His solid strokes told you he could play all day and into the night. He was a real jock.

Ed Collins didn't call Lester a genius for lobbing his way to victory, but he did take him aside at the end of the workshop for a chat, which included a back-handed invitation to come back next week and talk about working together on a clinic or two. Lester said thank you, Mr. Ed, but he had plenty of work. Lester did not mention his tennis elbow, caused by too much teaching. And fresh in the forefront of Lester's memory there was the shining example of the tireless red-bearded instructor. That dude was pure tennis, pure tenacity, a born jock. Beside this guy, Lester was a fake mannequin. He loved learning the tricks of the game. He wished for a different anatomy—and an athlete's x-ray vision.

NOONTIME MESSENGER—THE TURBULENT LIFE OF A TENNIS PRO

Armed with knowledge from three big-time tennis gurus, Lester forged himself into the outward form of a tennis pro. He wore white. He trimmed his beard. In the night chill, he wore a tennis sweater, white with red and blue piping along the collar. He wore an elbow brace for his tennis elbow. For the group classes at University Heights, Lester applied his knowledge gleaned from three tennis schools. He was over-educated. He was not a jock. He felt right at home.

He taught at night and one morning a week. He was just finishing up with a women's group—intermediates, the rankings before the advent of USTA ratings—when he got a visitor in a panel truck. His visitor was John L., a beginner in Lester's Tuesday evening class.

John L. was short and powerful. He was a busy man. He had taken the time out of his workday to bring Lester a message. He looked serious. He said to Lester:

"Hey man, you keep dealing this attitude, you're not gonna make it as a tennis teacher. You are way too sarcastic, you are not aware that you're out amongst the public, that your smart remarks turn everyone off.

"These people come to learn," he said. "They come to have fun. They pay their money, they take time out of their lives. They need help. They don't need your sarcasm."

Lester was stunned. And embarrassed. His irony, imported from the Beloit classroom, slid through him like an icicle. That same stuff that worked on college kids made this working man not want to show up for his tennis class once a week.

And Lester took the advice.

※ ※ ※

Instead of perfecting the caustic Drill Sergeant Mode, Lester shifted into Helpful Monk Mode. He got to be a better teacher. The students responded with grateful smiles.

Because of John the Noontime Messenger, Lester's tennis teaching improved. Students in his classes told their tennis friends. The friends told their friends. His group-lessons had waiting lists. People with money took private lessons without wanting to learn tennis. And Lester still had to deal with hotshot males in fancy cars who signed up for an hour lesson and started off playing a set, hoping to beat the Coach.

So Lester fed them his spins. Jerked them around. Changed speeds on the balls, sucked them in with his drop shot, then fed them the lob and yelled "That's your ball! Kill it!" Lesson after lesson, these wealthy interlopers, white ice cream shorts, shiny male neckwear, deep B-Movie film-star tans—could not get set up for the kill. For these guys, Lester developed a topspin lefty serve that bounced high to the backhand. Most of his big hitters needed a ball fed into their wheelhouse, halfway between the knees and the gut. Not very many had a high backhand return.

For Lester, these lessons were win-lose. He always won the set. He always lost a customer. He always got sweaty, so he brought fresh tennis shirts to the court. He seldom got a tip.

Men were tough to teach—guys in their late forties. They

were bored, they wanted to beat up on someone. They didn't care about tennis, the feel of the ball, the arc of the trajectory.

Lester's best students were women and kids. And while he was getting to be a better teacher, his body was betraying him. His tennis elbow was a permanent fixture. His knees ached at night. He needed a reason to keep going. He signed up for a weekend with Timothy Gallwey.

BOUNCE-HIT WITH TIMOTHY GALLWEY

Lester's fourth tennis school experience was the Inner Game, developed by Timothy Gallwey, a lean tennis genius born in San Francisco and captain of the Harvard tennis team. The term "inner game" was a metaphor for concentration, how to focus your brain. Not only on tennis, but on life. Gallwey's book, *The Inner Game of Tennis*, has sold over a million copies.

The Inner Game workshop took place in Tarzana, northwest of Los Angeles. It started on Friday and ended on Monday. Gallwey himself was not there to welcome his Saturday students—he was busy coaching a covey of corporation execs in a real-world version of the Inner Game—so Lester's group worked with a team of dedicated disciples, all devotees of the Inner Game method, which splits the tennis player into Self One and Self Two.

Self-One is the exterior competitor, a hard-hitting, score-keeping, blood-crazy killer who curses when he misses, blaming himself or his partner or his coach for not playing good enough to beat all comers. If you smash your racket on the court, no worries. That's just Self One out of focus.

To balance the mechanical fury of Self-One, you turn to the practical approach of Self-Two, the inner player, filled with anxiety and fear of losing. The key to playing satisfactory tennis is allowing Self Two to observe what happens when Self One hits the ball.

The focus of the Inner Game method is the art of focus itself. Not only keeping your eye on the ball, but also keeping your mind on the ball. The first drill on that first day was called *Bounce-Hit*. How simple it was.

When you drop the ball to start a rally, you say Bounce. When your strings contact the ball, you say Hit. When the ball you just hit touches down in the enemy court across the net, you say Bounce—the drill forces you to cross the net—when the enemy strings contact the ball, you say Hit.

At the Gallwey workshop, the students shouted out the words Bounce and Hit, a chorus of Inner Selves rejoicing in instant success on the court. On the court playing social doubles with your friends, you whisper the words to yourself. When the enemy serves, you say Hit. When the ball touches down in your service court, you say Bounce. When you return the ball, you say Hit.

※ ※ ※

The Gallwey Method encouraged learning while you were playing a match. Bounce-Hit is a silent meditation. Not even your partner needs to know. Lester had a friend who bounced the ball six to eight times before serving. Instead of going crazy, blaming his buddy for wasting court time, Lester counted off the bounces. One. Two. Three. Four. Five. Six. Seven. Hit.

Clock-Face.

The most complex drill at Gallwey's tennis symposium was Clock-Face, the 12 numbers of the day welded to the tennis ball you are hitting. To turn the ball into a clock-face, you flatten the roundness into a wafer, 12 o'clock at the top, 6 o'clock at the bottom, 3 o'clock on the right hand side, 9 o'clock on the left. If you are left-handed, you focus on 7-11. (Aside: Lester had seen very few left-handers with bad serves. It was almost as if the left-handed player exited the womb with a fully formed serve. So many right-handers had trouble playing against left-handers.)

If you are right-handed, and you want more slice on your serve, your strings contact the ball somewhere between 5 o'clock and 3 o'clock. If you are serving right-handed, you call out the clock face where your strings make contact, and then you observe the path of the ball.

The key word is observe—you are training the Eye of your Inner Self-Two to track the ball without adding judgment (good serve, lousy serve, stupid serve).

When your Self One makes contact with the ball, then Self-Two is engaged. If your strings make contact at 2 o'clock and the ball hits the net tape, Self-Two allows Self-One to make an adjustment on the next serve, or not. Self-One is the super sensitive ego. Self Two, the super-ego, must keep in control.

During the service lesson, the students stood in groups of six along the baseline. The server would serve, then call out the location on the clock face where the strings made contact with the side of the ball.

A contact at one o'clock, near twelve at the top of the ball, sent the serve into the net.

A contact at five o'clock sent the ball over the net and sometimes out of the court.

A contact at three o'clock, dragging the strings <u>across</u> the ball, added sidespin.

❋ ❋ ❋

If you were young enough to initiate a good back bend on the serve, your strings could make contact at six o'clock, the racket face brushing up from left to right, sending your serve into the backhand corner with a reverse spin into the receiver's backhand side, shoulder-high and hard to return. Did the six o'clock contact point contain the secret of topspin and the American Twist?

Targeting with Numbers.

The clock-face drill allows Self Two to meditate—and to mediate—with numbers. Using those numbers, Self-Two can nudge Self-One to find a target. This one is hard to believe until it works for you. Here's how you try it.

Set up a target across the net, say an empty tennis ball can. Practice your serve first. Place your target six inches in front of the service line. If you want to practice crosscourt, put the target on the singles sideline. If you want to practice hitting down the T, put the target there. Lester's first target was a can of tennis balls. These days, for his lessons, Lester uses orange plastic discs.

Self-One serves the first ball. Then Self Two, with no expectation of hitting the target, calls out the trajectory: one foot over, one foot to the left.

For example, if your ball landed three feet to the left, Self-Two says "three feet to the left." If your second ball sails over the target, Self-Two says, "twelve inches above." If your third ball connects, Self-Two reports the hit. "On Target." The server's job is to stay calm, not to be competitive in a blood-thirsty way. (Aside: When Lester is losing in doubles, he gets short of breath. He comes close to double-faulting. If he remembers to think back to the weekend with Timothy Gallwey and the Inner Game, Lester realizes that he has not practiced enough with the targeting exercise. Call yourself a Tennis Fool. Or a fool for tennis. Grin. Laugh. You are alive and not dead.)

❋ ❋ ❋

Gallwey himself appeared on Sunday. Lester saw him first on the show court, playing a flawless set with an enigmatic attendee named Jerry X, a super-good player who only showed up on Sunday, so he could cross sword-rackets with Gallwey the Legend.

They were lean men about the same age, still not showing their years, flirting with an entry into Middle Age, but cavorting with the style of great athletes. Perfect strokes, solid hits, heat on one shot, a subtle knuckle-ball curve on the next. Lester didn't know who won the set, who beat who, according to the score. But the way they played, you didn't care about the score. Because they were both magnificent.

After the exhibition, Gallwey hosted a Q and A session, still in his tennis whites, calm, not needing to sell his Inner Game Workshop, but just there, a tennis guru talking about the Center of Gravity (COG) that allowed everyone to hit better shots, to live a balanced life. He was three years younger than Lester, but he had the poise and the weighty demeanor of a Himalayan Guru. Gallwey was very direct. No waste motion. Good sense of humor. He had taken time out from retro-fitting corporate America, not only to check out his sub-teachers, but also just to be there. Presence. Showing up.

When the Inner Game workshop was over, Lester got good results from using the techniques in his teaching, especially Bounce-Hit. It worked every time, helping students to set their critical minds aside, letting their bodies enjoy playing tennis.

DESPERATELY SEEKING THE NEW MRS. LESTER

Since the departure of his ex-wife to the Hippy commune in Sausalito, Lester had dated a few women. Some were attractive.

Unlike Mrs. Lester (a lifetime student, a brilliant editor), these real-world women had real-world jobs. A couple of them were divorced. They had kids. Lester gave some of the kids tennis lessons. Dating took time away from his tennis, his novel-in-progress. Seven women later and he hadn't clicked with anyone.

Maybe Lester was in the wrong country. Maybe he should emigrate to Europe, retake French 101, teach tennis on the red clay in Nice or Grasse.

Laughable Aside: (In 13 French 101 classes, distributed across two decades, Lester never made it to French 102.)

❈ ❈ ❈

He was looking at flights to Paris when he signed up for a weekend of Encounter Grouping, built on the work of Carl Rogers, a psychologist whose theories about acceptance and empathy and genuineness had launched the person-centered workshop—just what Lester needed—which was taking place on the University of California, La Jolla, where a dozen attendees, shadow-boxing with early middle age, sat on mattresses in spartan student dorms and talked about their problems while trying to listen to their fellow reluctant middle agers talking about their problems.

Lester had not dwelt on his problems. He was not the brooding sort. He was not angry with his wife. She had her seven-year calendar and he was living the tennis life, playing good tennis, using good teaching tools. He'd made new friends. But sitting in that Spartan dorm room, listening to people opening up, spilling their problems onto strangers, Lester spoke up too.

And people listened. And he was surprised that people listened, and across from him—he was sitting on a thin student mattress, shoes off, back against the wall—and across from him were these two bare feet.

And the toes were wagging at Lester, some kind of semaphoric code.

The toes were signaling Hello.

The toes were attached to the feet of a woman, a gorgeous blonde in a pale blue blouse and tailored blue slacks. She was nodding as Lester talked. Nodding like she was listening. Like she cared. She looked like the actress Kim Novak.

* * *

When Lester finished she gave him a look of understanding and acceptance. She was allowing him to be himself. Her name tag said MP.

Around the room, people responded to Lester's plight.

He spent too much time alone.

He sounded stuck.

He needed someone in his life to help him get unstuck.

Name tag MP was nodding. In her eyes—they were Hazel—

Lester saw empathy and forgiveness.

When the time came for a lunch break, Lester waited outside the room for the name tag MP. When she came out, she said, "Are you waiting for me?" Lester felt a tingle. Her voice was warm, soft, engaging, just a touch of subtle humor. He invited her to lunch. Four other people asked: where do you eat around here? Lester was a local—he knew La Jolla. He drove them in his white Plymouth station wagon to a downstairs eatery, where MP, the blonde with the semaphoric feet, bought wine for the table, and Lester thought: This woman has money.

In the afternoon session, Lester tried to return the empathy he had received in the morning. It was not easy. Lester was not an empath. But he listened and he said thank you to the room of strangers and when the session had ended he invited MP to dinner.

She had a date.

Of course, she did.

* * *

But then they had a quick kiss in the elevator and when the kiss was over she invited him for breakfast. And after breakfast they strolled around the campus and Lester pointed out some gargoyles.

The gargoyles led to Paris and Notre Dame.

MP said she had never been out of the country.

They exchanged telephone numbers.

The beautiful MP took her classic semaphoric toes north to Orange County.

She lived in Newport Beach.

That meeting in the Carl Rogers Encounter group swerved Lester into a new life. One weekend he drove north to Newport Beach. The next weekend MP came down to San Diego.

Lester had a decision to make.

He was newly in love with MP.

He had built a life in San Diego—90 miles away, too far for a daily commute.

And sometimes Life has a way of unveiling the path. Doors swing open. New trails beckon, shimmering. And what did the new trails mean for his hard-earned tennis career?

PART VI

LIKE ANY SAVVY OLD PERSON, LESTER DENIES OLD AGE

TEACHING TENNIS AND GETTING OLD

Three real-world events quelled Lester's lust to be a full-time teaching pro. First, he pulled a muscle in his right calf. He stumped around with a cane for six weeks. He had to cancel lessons. He could not play Friday evening social tennis. He felt old age closing in. What if the tear had been worse? What would happen to his tennis teaching income?

Second, he consulted a career counselor supplied free by the city of San Diego—downtown in a rusty adobe building in a cluttered office where the guy gave him aptitude tests that were not only free, but also fun—and illuminating.

The tests defined Lester's sojourn into tennis as a long siesta.

You've been asleep, the counselor said. Now you're waking up. Time to get back to your waking life. You had an enviable rest. Feel good, feel lucky. Get with it.

Third, Lester consulted Coach BP, a big-name tennis pro, famous across Southern California. They met for breakfast in a San Diego diner. Lester was seeking advice that would affect the rest of his life. He was happy to pay the tab.

❊ ❊ ❊

Coach BP was a San Diego native. He had played against Jack

Kramer, Pancho Gonzales, Bobby Riggs and Bill Tilden. He grew up in University Heights, where Lester, years later, was running the city parks tennis program. Coach BP had coached Maureen Connelly, first woman to win the Grand Slam (Australia, France, England, United States)—when she was only 18. Coach BP had also worked with Karen Hantze Susman, who won both singles and doubles at Wimbledon—her doubles partner was Billie Jean (Moffitt) King.

When they met for breakfast, Lester had been certified by the USPTA (United States Professional Teaching Association) and the USPTR (United States Professional Tennis Registry). He had joined the local chapter of teaching pros. He was torn between San Diego, where his friends and lessons lived, and Orange County, where MP, his blonde sweetie, had a major super-sonic real-world career at UC-Irvine. Spearing a chunk of pancake, Coach BP said: to make it as a teaching pro in today's tennis environment, you need your own facility.

At the magic word *facility*, Lester's tidy make-believe world collapsed:

Facility implied ownership.

Ownership meant real estate.

Real estate meant Pro Shop.

Pro Shop meant Inventory—rackets, balls, strings, stringing machine, grips.

Real Estate meant Tennis courts—upkeep, re-surfacing.

Accident insurance.

Debt.

Monthly payments.

Bank loans.

Pressure.

Employee problems.

Customer relations.

Marketing and PR.

Desolation.

A back-breaking load on Lester's narrow aging shoulders.

* * *

The two tennis pros finished breakfast. They shook hands. When Coach BP learned that Lester was headed for Europe, he invited him for a visit to a real tennis facility— the Hotel Coronado—where he was head pro, and where Lester got a life-changing on-court lesson—in humility.

Coach BP had invented the Scepter, the first tennis racket made of graphite. When Lester arrived, the sun was retreating westward, sinking into the ocean. The empty tennis courts echoed.

Coach BP handed Lester a demo model of the Scepter. He said: since you're getting in early, Lester, you can represent us in Europe.

<u>Us</u> meant the business of selling Scepters to the French, the Italians, Serbs and Croats, the Brits.

The simple word <u>Us</u> made Lester nervous.

Coach BP possessed a Swoosh forehand.

The ease of the Swoosh forehand told Lester that Coach BP had started playing in early childhood.

He'd won matches in high school and college.

He'd had a taste of the big time—trophies and big name partners—and here he was, hitting to a non-jock dreamer on this shadowy tennis court—a dreamer who would always be an intruder in the company of a bone fide tennis pro.

The way he handled the tennis ball told Lester that Coach BP was a born jock.

Early childhood lessons.

A temporary toehold in the big time.

A deadly Swoosh forehand. Easy swing, zero effort.

Coach BP was the real thing.

Lester handed over forty bucks, the demo price for the Scepter. He shook hands with Coach BP, who wished Lester luck in Europe. The Coach went back to his Pro Shop. Lester drove across the bridge to the PLTC. And then, still remembering his amateur performance with Coach BP, he drove north to University City, where he tried to be less sardonic in his lesson for beginners.

* * *

In Europe, Lester played two times with the Scepter. He lost both times. The Scepter was head-heavy. Lester was traveling light. He left the Scepter with tennis friends in Italy.

He met MP in Paris.

She landed with a plane-load of U.S cops—chiefs, sheriffs, marshals—here in this historic town to learn crowd-control tactics from the Paris police department. At that time, Paris had a police force of 25,000 officers.

After Paris, Lester and the beautiful MP took the train to Amsterdam.

Then to Switzerland. Denmark. Norway, where MP had family. Austria. Italy. France and Mt. St. Michel. London. Home.

* * *

Lester and MP bought a condo in Irvine, a town-house facility called Woodbridge. Twenty tennis courts. They set up house-keeping, tussled about closet space and dresser drawers. MP helped Lester understand the basics in his first desk-top computer. MP got Lester a job teaching in the UCI school of extension, the adult learner program. He was back in the classroom, teaching adults how to write better, how to see the bones of literature. Without the pressure of faculty committees (indelible memories from his time at Beloit), Lester enjoyed classroom teaching. Life was good.

He asked for the hand of the beautiful MP.

She said Yes.

They got a license in Taos, New Mexico.

They got married in an outdoor chapel on a mountain looking down on Eagle Nest, New Mexico.

They honey-mooned in Santa Fe.

Lester was not alone anymore.

LESTER'S LAST TENNIS LESSON

The Woodbridge town-house where he lived with Mrs. Lester (the radiant MP) was a half-mile from Irvine Valley College, where Lester joined a choir, where he made sure to sit next to a baritone with a good voice who could read music.

Despite his enforced childhood piano lessons, and despite singing in choirs since he was fourteen, Lester could not read music—so he always sat next to a math guy or an engineer—those guys could read like Mozart—so Lester would listen hard, follow along, get a feel for tempo and nuance, and have the bass-baritone part memorized by performance time.

Lester envied these guys who could read notes, these Miraculous Music Men, and this one was named Sal, so when he learned about Lester being an ex-tennis teacher he offered to pay for lessons, but Lester reciprocated with a freebie.

He owed Sal—who made it possible for Lester to sing.

* * *

Woodbridge had 20 first-rate tennis courts—newish nets, superior lighting for night-time play. Lester reserved Court seven, way down the line, away from the pro shop. Sal's eye for tennis did not match his ear for music, but he was strong and fast and eager, and Lester owed him, big time, and people kept stopping to watch the lesson—the ball hopper, the routines, Lester all in white—and three mothers outside the fence begging him to teach their children.

Lester was tempted. He loved teaching. He did okay with kids. With these eager moms, Lester could build a business teaching tennis. But then he recalled his chilly grey weekday morning where he bought breakfast for Player-Teacher-Coach BP, back in San Diego.

Coach BP's words echoed—you need your own facility.

The curtain slammed down—again. Teaching tennis was no longer a lark. It was a business. And being in the tennis business would land Lester in the World of Business: licenses, re-certification, income and income taxes. Staffing. Competition from other pros, advertising yourself by playing in tournaments.

And Lester's elbow was hurting.

And his wrist.

He tracked both pains backward into his uneven tennis past: late lessons, wood rackets, the rigid Don Budge forehand.

So Lester said no thanks to the eager moms. He was teaching writing at U-Cal Irvine, night school for adults. He was into writing now, a detective series set in Orange County. He was taking a marketing course at Irvine Valley College, trying to understand the arcane antics amongst book publishers.

The marketing teachers were small business gurus. Two weeks into the term, Lester saw the need for a textbook— starting your small business. The twin business gurus agreed.

Through his publishing contacts, Lester sent the book around. It was snapped up by a major publisher. And Lester got lucky with his editor—a savvy higher up guy on his way to the top.

Lester was having fun.

That book—*Small Business: An Entrepreneur's Plan*—lasted through multiple revisions.

Writing books kept Lester off the tennis court for two decades.

Cause and effect.
Economics.
Supply and demand.
The tennis clock ticking softer, slowing down.

THE ART OF DENIAL

While Lester was busy with his writing—cranking out self-help books like The Weekend Novelist—Mrs. Lester, the beautiful MP, landed a big-time whopper career-raising job—Director of Personnel (soon to become Human Resources) at the University of Washington in Seattle.

At this point in his tennis life, Lester was ignoring the signs of old age.

Losing to younger players.

Slowing down on the court.

Hitting softer because he didn't have the muscle.

Crappy footwork.

More exaggerated spin balls.

In California, two decades ago, Lester had tennis buddies and 20 courts just up the street. In Seattle, Lester had two beat-up Soundview courts, wet with rain, heavy with pine needles.

Where was Lester's next A-Team?

❋ ❋ ❋

He got killed in tournaments—those pesky young guys. To keep his timing, he offered free coaching to his new Adult Learning boss at University Extension. He was grateful that he could still hit a teaching ball. He still ached for his own A-Team. And he was still drifting away from the game when he got diagnosed with prostate cancer, a PSA of 8.3—danger zone territory—and spent three weeks researching treatment.

Treatments for prostate cancer rippled across the internet. Seeds hot with radioactivity. Cryotherapy—freeze those varmints. Chemo-therapy and its side-effects: nausea, vomiting, fatigue, neuropathy, constipation, Diarrhea.

Radiation—28 trips to the hospital to get zapped—and then your cells are pumped full of radiation..

Three weeks of research on treatment included consultations with 9 medical professionals.

Four medical doctors.

Five naturopaths.

One doc, a hotshot MD eager to prove himself and his product, commanded Lester to go with the seeds. Three other docs said surgery.

One naughty naturopath, a hotshot, commanded Lester to subject himself to chemo—his motive was profit, snatching up another customer.

The other four naturopaths said surgery.

Back in those days, there was no miracle treatment, like the focal lase ablation of today. Spooked, Lester saw Death astride a pale horse. Fear gripped his throat. Darkness up ahead. The end.

Lester chose surgery.

✳ ✳ ✳

The surgeon did well: We got it all, he said. Including 9 lymph nodes.

Lester was weary, he was swollen, he was constipated, but still alive at 64—one year away from sliding over into Senior Tennis—but he was too weak to climb stairs. And then he twisted his knee on a stair-stepper machine at the gym, trying to get back in shape. A recuperatory visit to France came too soon. Lester used a cane, tapping on the sidewalks of Paris, the village pathways of Provence. He had never felt older.

Stair steps were trouble. His stamina went fast. Was this old age? His face looked ancient. He watched tennis on TV. He would never play again. He threw himself into teaching. He rejoined the Natalie Goldberg writing group at Louisa's Bakery and Café. He wrote a book about prostate cancer that no publisher wanted. He chatted about tennis with a new writer, Player ZH, actor, showman, commentator, voice of Seattle football.

Player ZH played tennis three times a week.

His tennis indoor HQ was Amy Yee.

It took him several tries to lure Lester back onto a tennis court.

They met at Soundview.

That same chilly day in January. Pale sun, leafless trees, dark water spots on the court. They hit short-court.

Lester kept missing.

He was late to the ball.

His timing was laughable.

But he loved the feeling.

He loved trying to swing.

He loved creating with his strings the magical arc of the ball.

He was slow. He was old. He was alive. His heart skipped a beat. He was back on the court. Moving to the ball. Sizing it up. After all these years, he was still not a jock.

But Lester still loved this game.

And maybe someday he could write the book about playing tennis even when you got old.

Playing with friends.

   Playing senior tennis.

Playing so you won't die.

APPENDIX ONE: THE BYRANT PARK THREESOME

Player LE met Players PH and JD in that first SD&P class at the TCSP. Player PH was the proud owner of the ever-enviable swoosh forehand. Player JD was fast—and her best kill shot was the forehand lob. She hit medium-paced balls, luring the enemy to the net, and then she drove her lob over the enemy heads, cries of disdain, out-stretched rackets flailing.

And on her face was this crafty smile.

Player JD is the driving force behind the Bryant Park Threesome. Her injury—falling off a ladder in her slant-hill garden; the doctor said she might never play tennis again—drove Player PH to form the group now known as the Bryant Park Threesome. They follow the lead of Billie Jean King, who traveled to Australia—her trip paid for by Aussie businessman Robert Mitchell—King needed Australia because the big-time American males refused to work out with women. In Australia, King trained under the great Australian coach Mervyn Rose—working out with players like Tony Roche and Fred Stolle.

A workout called Three—two against one, rotate.

* * *

1. Warming Up, Senior Style

The Threesome starts in the short court. They focus on footwork, bumping the ball, chipping, keeping the ball inside the service lines. Player JD to PH to LE and back to JD. They focus on consistency, not power. Teamwork, not killing the ball. Good footwork forces them into the ready position, mindful of the COG (Center of Gravity)—feet apart, knees bent, both hands on the racket. Mixed with huffs and puffs, there is chit-chat. What happened yesterday. The day before. Anyone remember the last SD&P?

The short court warm-up came from Dennis Van Der Meer, his classes for adult club players, attended eons ago by both Player PH and Player LE. As the warm-up comes to an end, the Threesome narrows the focus. Let's do volleys. Let's hit serves. Let's do serve-and-return.

❋ ❋ ❋

2. Serving Practice: ORIENT YOUR SERVE BY Backing Up

To practice the serve, the threesome starts on the service line, hitting down into the service court across the net. When you stand up close, it's easy to slam the ball into the enemy court. When they are all serving 100 per cent, the threesome moves back to the 60-foot line (a better name for "No Man's Land"), halfway between the service line and the baseline.

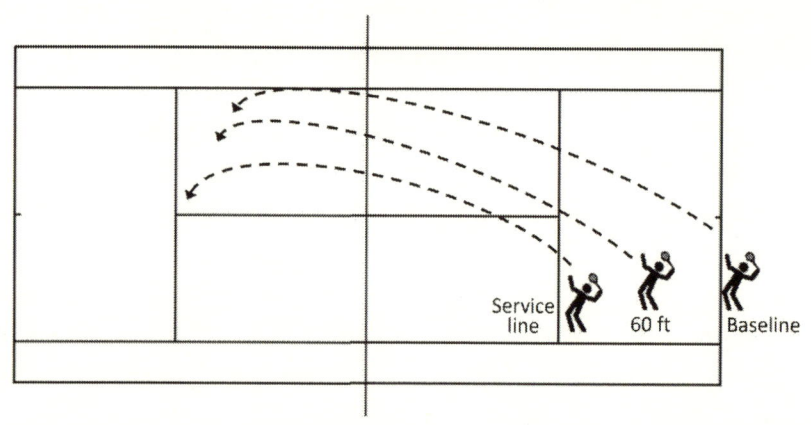

[Diagram of tennis court showing three players at baseline serving toward service box, with labels "Service line", "60 ft", and "Baseline"]

Success in this drill is hitting the court without tagging the net or going long. No coach needed. When all three players have the range from the 60-foot line, they move farther back to the base line. They hit harder now—the ball has farther to go. If the success rate falls, then all three players focus on the spin needed to bring the service ball down into the court. Some service balls slap the tape. Some balls go long, past the service line. Some go wide. This drill informs the server, without using words, that a correction is needed. It's that kind of knowledge—learned together, over and over—that allows them to work together as a team. When everyone knows the secret, then there's only the need for reminders.

No coach needed.

Serving practice continues with all three players hitting until someone wants to receive. Because of the morning sun, the servers take the north court. The returner returns from the south. The returner is a stand-in for the enemy. The enemy represents competition. Do the servers try to hit aces? Does the returner try to hit winner-returns? Do the servers want their shots returned so that they can play the point out?

The threesome always takes a moment to work through the possibilities. Some days the servers want to hit hard and deep. Some days the returner wants to hit winner returns. So it's smart to state goals before starting the drill. If the servers are foaming at the mouth—a sign they want to hit aces—then the simplest calming solution is to aim at a target. For example, aim one ball at the corner. Aim the next ball at the T.

*** * * ***

Apply the same strategy if the returner wants to kill every return.

Decide on a target. You can serve cross-court, aiming at the ad court corner, or serve down the line, aiming at the service T —to make sure the return is reachable by the returner. Or you can serve to the deuce court corner—into the right-hander's backhand.

After a dozen serves the threesome breaks for water. Player LE munches a chocolate bar. He is the oldest and the weakest. He runs out of energy first. They do their best not to mock him. Play or Die, Lester, but not right here, not in the sun and summer shade of Bryant Park. At least wait until the threesome has its coffee and pastries.

3. VOLLEY DRILLS

There are three fat immovable targets in tennis: ad court, deuce court, and the center line Tee. Your goal as a senior doubles player is to set up your partner with a shot that leaves one of those targets empty. If your first shot pushes one enemy player back and wide, your partner volleys the ball between the two enemies. If you lob your service return over the enemy net player (don't hug the net, don't guard the alley) then you're setting your partner up for an easy kill.

To move from the baseline into the court, Seniors need to volley better. If your volley needs work, if you need a radical approach based on obvious common sense, then check the very doable volley drills on "Feel Tennis" on YouTube—developed by Tomaz, the droll Slovenian professional of Feel Tennis, who offers an amazing number of free videos.

Tomaz is smart and persuasive and wry. And he's really easy

to locate. Head over to YouTube and type in this directive: "How to develop good hands at the net"—where you will see on your screen a couple of limber teenagers—students of Tomaz—being taught to slow the rally down with a stop-and-catch technique that starts with trapping the ball on the string-bed—which trains any random semi-normal old person to feel the ball.

And to hit better volleys.

When everyone has volleyed, the threesome winds up the workout by playing short-court—returning to the same drill as the warm-up—but this time they play two against one—and this time they keep score. The rules: the ball can bounce only once. No volleys allowed. That means if you have charged the net, and you get a ball floating ball hit right at you, then you don't have room to let the ball bounce. You lose the point.

SHORT COURT

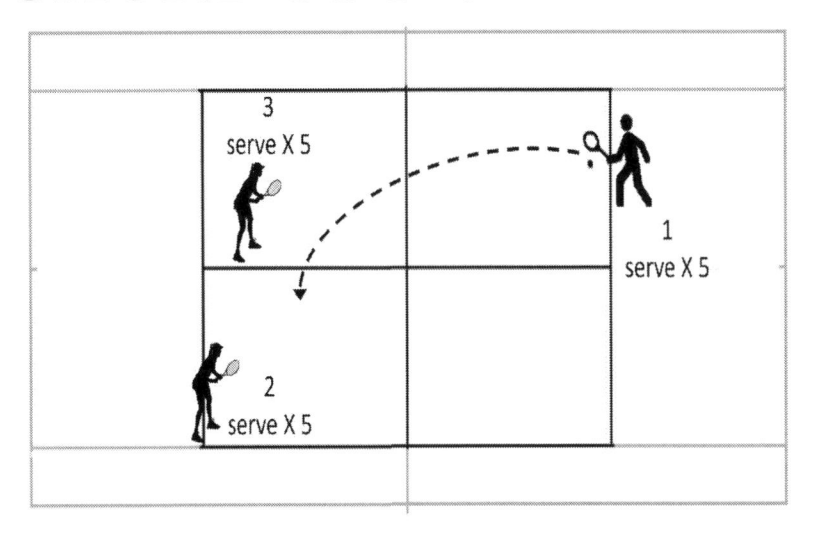

I n short court, the single defender serves first, five balls sliced or pushed or bumped across the net, into the corners. The enemy attacker serves five balls from the deuce court. The attacker's partner serves five balls from the ad court. The winner is first to 15. Rotate.

Short court is great for seniors because they don't have to race for the shots. They have already practiced their match serves, and now they have to hit an underhand serve. Short court is all about direction and finesse. Serving underhand trains the players to direct the ball to the corners. Short court tennis trains the feet.

To return most balls, you have to lower your COG (Center of

Gravity), which trains your footwork. Some short court players are gripped by the need for speed. A few short court failures could change that player's life. The best shot for short court is the soft slice, dripping with spin. Since a player can't take the ball in the air, a team of two can use soft mini-lobs to push their opponent back behind the service line, and then win the point with a drop shot. The hitter controls the altitude.

※ ※ ※

If you play short court and don't know how to hit soft spin, you will learn fast. It's all about slowing down. Short court also trains the eyes. When you're down there close to the court surface, and the enemy ball sinks down, you can see the magic of spin up close. If your feet need training, the spinning ball will train your feet and your reflexes and your sense of direction—where to hit your next shot. In short court, you seldom get all flustered with panic.

PLAYER JD AND HER CROSS-CULTURAL MUSINGS

Tennis players have a verbal mantra, "Watch the ball! Watch the ball!"

Fishermen/women have a descriptive phrase, "We catch and release."

But what about the word, Threesome:

T-hree is an odd number with which to comprise a team, but a team we be.
H-aving coffee after workout a must. Cookies, pie, croissants from PCC our choices.
R-elearning good form requires unlearning old. Turn the body, straighten the arm, keep low, watch the ball.
E-very workout has a routine: warm-up, serving, return of serve, volleying, short court accuracy.
E-very week our "boss" adapts the routine to work on deficiencies discovered in that week's play.
S-ense of hopelessness is unacceptable. Sense of humor unshakable.
O-ld but not too old is our motto.
M-eeting and sometimes squeegeeing, sweeping,

*toweling, leveling signs. Then the good part...hitting **E**-nergy used generates optimism. We can always improve.*

PLAYER PH AND HIS RHYMES

When he hits a really fine Swoosh forehand, Player PH gives a series of whoops, creating a soundtrack for the warm-up—impossible to reproduce on the page. Players PH and LSM Lester had excellent work-outs on the Soundview Courts, but the Threesome is more interesting. Player PH, an aficionado of opera and showbiz tunes, chats about the letter Three:

Player PH:

What is it about three? I think of Sondheim's lyrics from "Company": "One's impossible, Two is dreary, Three is company, Safe and cheery"

Three is bad for scoring, but good for practice.

Lots of volleys, two against one, but rotating regularly so no one gets too tired. If we were four, it would turn into a game with points. Instead we just hit. The emphasis is on focus, tone, consistency. Can we go 10 hits without missing? 20?

Often we coach each other. "The ball was down, your eyes were up." "Turn more." "Change your grip." "Higher toss needed on that serve." If we can remember the drill, we'll re-run an exercise from the last class with Coach MB.

In the winter, we sopped up the water-pools with towels and Player JD's magical squeegee. In the summer, we met early, beating the sun. Bryant Park has two courts. If we're on Court One, there's a serious doubles game happening on Court Two. It's a family park, a people's park where kids and grown-ups shoot baskets at two hoops just outside the tennis fence. On the eastern side, toddlers, dogs, mommies.

Workouts for the Threesome last an hour and fifteen minutes. Two breaks, maybe three. Then we use the hopper to pick up balls —each branded with Player LE's jocular magic marker dollar sign —and stride up the hill and across the street to the safety of the PCC. Player JD drags a third metal chair over to a table on the south wall. Players PH and LE go inside to forage for coffee and munchies: cookies for LE, a muffin for PH, and always a slice of berry pie for JD. There is talk.

That's it: "Three is company, safe and cheery."

After tennis chit-chat: travel memories, travel plans upcoming. Books. Films. Gossip. Tennis talk from the ancient brains kept sharp by the miraculous stroking of the tennis ball.

APPENDIX TWO: OF TENNIS, THEY DO SING

Tennis players are poetic souls. They play a beautiful game. Often they turn to words about tennis. They are not alone. Edward de Vere, a spoiled and naughty 16th century hanger-on in the Court of Queen Elizabeth, penned a cute sonnet about the game of tennis. Here's the opening ploy:

> When as the heart at tennis plays, and men to gaming fall,
> Love is the court, hope is the house, and favour serves the ball.

When he was halfway through the first draft of *Play or Die*, Lester asked his tennis friends for writings on the game—poetry or prose—and here's what he got:

1. Player MTS—a student of Coach MB.
2. Player ZH—a Leftie with a poem..
3. Player ME—a Leftie with a mean lob.
4. Player TA—with his doubles partner, Player JW—these heavy hitters took on a pair of youngsters half their combined age.

OBJECTS ARE FARTHER THAN THEY APPEAR: LIGHTNING AMONG THE RECTANGLES

By Player MTS

Player MTS is the proud owner of a deceptive Swoosh forehand. He seldom misses. He possesses a ton of tenacity. He enjoys creating analogies. He sees himself as a backcourt player, but if you play against him, he seems always to be at the net, crowding in on your space, slamming a forehand volley.

    1. I have often felt grateful that I once read about self-driving cars: passengers are always scared that other objects, including other cars, appear too close. There might seem to be only two millimeters separating you from the car in the next lane, but it's perfectly safe. That fact reassures me sometimes when my eyesight is feeling fear while driving. As I grow older, that fear increases, and a similar fear can affect me when I'm playing doubles tennis. The ball feels too close and I move back; my partner feels too close and I back off.

    2. I learned better, not only from my reading, but also from

a moving van. On a Friday morning I headed out in my car for tennis. A small moving van in the apartment building's parking lot looked as if it might block my exit. There was a very narrow possible opportunity between it and a parked car. I asked one of the men carrying furniture out of the truck, "Do you think I can fit through there?"

We decided to fold in the side mirrors on the car and the truck and give it a try. Of course, he could have moved the truck, but we both seemed to be willing to navigate this tiny Northwest Passage. If I had not previously learned that objects seemingly too close to self-driving cars are farther than they appear, I never would have trusted a van-moving-man to guide me with precise hand motions and well-chosen words. Even though I knew objects appear closer than they really are, and even though I could see clearly how far I was from (how close I was to) the van on my left (50 mm or less), I was still hesitant to move farther left when directed to do so. Faith and knowledge overcame fearful perception. I had never driven that close to anything in my life.

Halfway through, he jokingly warned, "There's no turning back now; you won't be able to back up." Surprisingly, I felt no claustrophobia. Since I'm alive now, you know I made it through.

3. Before getting to the tennis lesson that will be the featured revelatory event of this essay, let me tell a snippet of tennis background. The previous Tuesday I had executed a controlled, powerful, precise volley, instinctively judging where the ball would be and stepping into it just right. My previous instincts have almost always been to be too careful, to move backwards inappropriately. My natural strength is defense.

At that moment, though, I was on full offense and my only caution was making sure that my partner HK's steps were not approaching me from behind. After all, the ball was traveling directly toward her, and I had to jump in front of her to hit a satisfyingly winning volley, possibly my best ever, which felt like an important milestone in my path to improving. One thing Coach MB had been hammering into me is how necessary it is to move forward and come up really close to the net, just short of rule-breakingly touching it, when conditions for a put-away are right. It always feels too close to me, but that one time maybe I had overcome my caution.

4. And on the featured Friday, it all became vivid; it all came to life in a new way. Usually we have four students in a typical Coach MB lesson. If we have only three, as we did this particular Friday, sometimes Coach MB will join in as a fourth. After we had done some three-ways drills, in which he fed us shots, he did join in like a real fourth. Even when he does join in, though, he usually holds back. I don't know how much he was holding back this time, but it sure seemed like not at all. Part of one pattern consisted of volleying short to the opponent's backhand and then immediately floating into position close to the net for the put-away that would almost certainly be available. More than once, showing us how, Coach MB jumped in front of HN. Fast, accurate, forward, surprising, near the net. Very near the net.

Now, let me tell you, HN is the fastest mover among the dozens of people I play tennis with, and I'm talking about many speedy 40-somethings as well as us 70-somethings. Yet, HN stood still as if he were shocked and glued, while Coach MB moved in between him and the net, where there were only a few millimeters, not enough for a person to fit into. And yet, fit in Coach MB did.

After having read long ago that objects are farther than they appear when you're riding in a self-driving car, and after having squeezed beside the stationary moving van, and after having stepped in front of HK to make a great volley, I got to see, up close and personal, some really great volleys in a space too small for a human. Three experiences had prepared me to see for the first time, after dozens and dozens of lessons, Coach MB playing apparently full-on, two meters from me. Part of any success is talent and experience, of course, but part is also not being unreasonably afraid, and part is trusting instincts based on learning that has been validated by coaches.

Precisely targeted tennis skill echoes, reverberates in a larger context of perception and proprioception in the physical world. Less fear. More invasion into small spaces. Bright sun breaking through cloudy haze. Lightning among the rectangles.

POETRY ON THE COURT
By Player ZH

Player ZH is the formidable friend (actor, announcer, writer) who lured Lester back into tennis. It took some persuasion—Lester felt old, his bones were creaky, he couldn't get to the ball, hitting the ball felt strange, not like the old days—but Player ZH persisted, and Lester's later years were brightened with senior tennis. Player ZH is a deadly player with a solid leftie forehand—he's also a poet. Here's his poem on Senior Tennis.

Senior tennis with aches and pains
missed opportunities and who's to blame
at the net points to be won
bottom line is we are having fun

Is it such an awful sin
in every games desire to win
competition makes me tick
with friends in my demographic

"Southpaw" "Lefty" that's what they say
as I walk on the court to play
a strategy is for all to land
deep fast blows to my backhand

*Ready myself to take the fight
knowing backhand is kryptonite
they look amazed at my shot so deft
forgetting they hit it to my left*

PLAYING TO THE LIMIT

By Player ME

P layer ME is another Leftie. Lester met him during Wednesday Senior Doubles (Geri's Group) on the courts at Lower Woodland, which are higher than the Upper Woodland Courts, and also farther north on the map of the Upper Woodland Court, an example of Seattle's confusing topsy-turvy naming of landmarks and streets.

Player ME has superior footwork.

I started playing tennis again after a very long break from it. Work not only has a way of limiting your time but your ability to see free time. When I retired, it took a while for me to get used to seeing free time. But here I am now. Retired. Turning 70 this year. Playing tennis, a lot. With other seniors, nearly every day of the week. Sometimes twice a day. Going on for more than a year now - and still reaching for more senior moments of consistency.

Speaking of consistency, it just doesn't happen by playing more. Playing more helps but, as a senior, I have learned that practice, by itself, does not make perfect. Progressive drill repetition with an instructor goes further but, as a senior, that still does not make perfect. What has motivated me to sustain the drive for more improvement is doubles' competition. Singles doesn't do it. When you miss a shot in doubles there is a partner you let down. There is also a team you let down. Having that partner relationship is key to applying the pressure to improve with every point. You want your partner to make that shot. If you don't make the next shot, and you lose the game, set or match, it will be seared on your memory long after the match. Nothing drives the motivation to improve like losing a doubles match that you should have won! For senior competition, we can go further. Nothing drives the motivation to improve like winning a doubles match that you almost lost!

Fast forward: Match Day for our over-65 team.

I am assigned the #3 doubles team with one of our most senior of backspin players. Wicked backspin. The kind of back spin that sticks on the ground before taking a radical turn away from your prepared ground stroke. After splitting sets 3-6, 6-2, I am asking myself, "how did we get to this 10-point tiebreaker? And why is my partner's hand bleeding?" In the senior moment of the tie break, I fail to recall whether we are down 2-5 or 2-7. Somehow, my partner and I get the tiebreak to a 7-7 tie. Then to 8-8. By this time, the other two courts are done and those doubles' players are starting to watch our final tiebreak points. 9-9. 10-10. We take the lead 11-10. Match point. Our serve. Good deep service return. Good backspin groundstroke is returned as a hard line-drive to my ready racket at the net. Minimum racket movement forehand volley contacts off-center that delivers the ball back to an empty back corner. 12-10! Match decided by the narrowest of margins.

FEARLESS SENIORS TEST THEMSELVES
Away from the Relative Safety of Senior Tennis
by Player TA

Player TA grew up on the East Coast. His athletic abilities drew him into the business of sports. Gyms, recreation clubs. He is a powerful player with a big forehand and he rushes the net after every serve. His purpose is to intimidate the enemy. He is best buddies with Player JW, who hits a murderous flattish forehand..

Evidence: When Lester tried to return a forehand hit by Player JW, he popped a tendon in his left wrist.

Player TA writes about a weekend tournament held indoors on TCSP courts. To level the playing field, the tournament draw arranged teams by combining their USTA rankings. Both Player TA and Player JW were 3.5's—their opponents had to match rankings—a total of 7.0. There was nothing in the match-ups about age—which team was younger; which team was older. Catch the action below.

Player TA narrates.
Almost 70 years of age BUT – not giving a damn about it.
Well that's how I have to feel every time I compete against anyone 20 or more years younger than me.
So when I asked Player JW to play with me in the TCSP club

tennis tournament, I figured if there's one guy that thinks about not giving a damn – it's Player JW .

I mean – what do we have to lose. Our combined ages = 135. Most of our opposition would most likely come in around 80 yrs of age.

Nervous?? – of course – so in our first match we drew a couple of guys that may have nudged their 80 to 90…big deal – who cares ? We have surprise on our side. As long as we continue to give the impression that they struck gold by playing two old timers, then all we have to do is make them think again.

Yes – we won our first match. No – we don't communicate with each other like they do on TV. No signals, no talking up close in between each point. Been playing tennis for over 50 years now – what the hell am I gonna say ? 'Gee if I hit my serve wide Player JW – go here, there and everywhere (my apologies to Lennon/McCartney)..

I know if I hit it hard on a serve or a return of serve these guys are gonna pop it up. Player JW will make them pay and if we do it enough times – they'll sulk.

Yep – that's what happened.

Sound cocky ? Once the nerves smooth out and we evaluate how good or not so good the opponents are – we'll be alright.

Next up we get two opponents in the 50-60 combined age group and we're told they are the favorites to win the whole thing. Spoiler alert – they did.

So I think to myself – let's get them thinking about the differences in age—let them worry about losing to guys more than twice (one of them 3x) their age. Put the pressure on them.

We lose the first set pretty handily. These youngsters are good and quick. Second set – we stage a comeback – bring it to 4-5 and we're on the brink. Player JW 's got fire in his eyes and yet – just wanting wasn't enough. We lose 4-6. The youngsters look relieved. We are OK with the loss – until the replay in our minds. The missed opportunities in the second set. What if we'd done this? What if we'd done that ?

My consolation – I tell the boys our combined ages and make

sure they know they were in a tough fight. Screw it I figured – why make them go home feeling 100% like victors. One thing my 69 years taught me is – you may beat me (tennis or otherwise) but you're gonna know you're not that HOT.

EPILOGUE: TO GET THERE

A TENNIS PILGRIM PILGRIMAGE

In the early half-dawn dark, the Tennis Pilgrim heads south to the stop sign, where he swings onto 85th with a swift left turn—headlights slashing the trees—no jagged dawnlight sun today, eager to blind him—goosing the Rav4 just ahead of the east-bound traffic, stopping for the red light at 15th, his driver's side mirror scant inches away from the rock-pocked yellowjacket dermis of a city bus, snugging into the right lane, while the maniac left turners edge forward, pawing the tarmac still winking with icicles from last night's freeze.

East on 85th, hugging the right lane, past Freddy's Greenwood store, making the light at First, slowing for Greenwood Avenue, waiting for the light—it lasts only 9 seconds—and then barreling up the hill past Dayton, Fremont, pushy gargantuan SUV in his rearview, hang a right at Linden, avoiding the bilious white service van crowding the narrow street packed with cars—skimpy surface street, fat vehicles—a rolling semi-stop for the 4-way on 83rd, hang a left down the hill, easing toward the curb to avoid getting clipped by a chubby white Cadillac wallowing up the hill, its left wheels way across the imaginary center line—a road bump slows him down, the Pilgrim sits second in line for the signal.

Count to fifteen, twenty-five, thirty-five.

Breathe.

The light goes green. The Rav4 angles across Aurora on a 45 degree turn, ambles down the trail on Greenlake Drive North, the speedometer locked down at 20 MPH, school zone speed, no children in sight, a traffic guard with a slow sign, the Rav4 brakes for 80th, spell out the numbers counting themselves down inside the little glass window mounted on the telephone pole at the awkward 5-street intersection of 80th, North Greenlake Drive, and Interlake.

He tests the radio.

NPR reporting on the Russians, the Proud Boys, the ex-president who would be Hitler-king.

Radio silence, the Pilgrim heads west again on 80th.

If the line of three cars goes thirty, he can make the light at Wallingford. But today is a day for tourists, newbies to the city, lost and wandering, making the Pilgrim pay.

He should head back home. Return to his starting place. This town is full up with newbies getting lost and screwing up what could be the last tennis pilgrimage. What if today is the last day?

Bagley, Corliss, Sunnyside.

Up the hill and across I-5, the great divider, the Pilgrim leaves behind the once all-Nordic bastion of beautiful Ballard —recent creatrix of massive traffic jams—heading south-east down Banner Way to 75th, where the nose of his vehicle presses into the dominion of Lower Lake City, Fairview, the Roosevelt Reservoir, Ravenna, Third Place Books, cueing in on the traffic —how many construction trucks, how many busses, how many soccer moms and their armloads of children—citizens of tomorrow, who will make it possible for the Pilgrim to slip-slide into even older age, with stolen moments of grace.

Back to the pilgrimage.

Major congestion on 75th dictates a right turn onto 25th, the Pilgrim hugging the left lane, speeders passing him on the right, their vehicles zipping past lit up by irritation because the

Pilgrim was going only 31 in a 25-mile zone and the speedy passers zipping by prove how important they are by driving like shit-heads.

The Pilgrim waits for the light.

He turns left onto 65th, crowded, but calmer than 75th.

Up the hill, the Bryant Corner Café, great coffee, exotic pastries—a compulsory stop on 35th while seven vehicles up in front try to turn left against the serious uphill traffic, forcing the Pilgrim to wait because today the extra curb space reserved for turning is blocked by a giant SUV, white, with Texas plates.

Morons—yet another reason for the Pilgrim to say goodbye, Texas.

Down the hill through the intersection feeling free.

Feeling his tennis reflexes stirring.

Pilgrim needs coffee.

He hauls a left onto 40th, then a right into the parking lot at the PCC. He masks up—locates his money-clip—and heads indoors, inhaling the cold wet morning air.

He nods at a sweeper.

The sweeper nods back.

The Pilgrim nods at a cashier.

She nods back.

He likes it here.

Feels right at home.

A watering hole on his Pilgrimage.

He waits in line for the super-meticulous detail-obsessed driver from the yellow-and-black school bus parked across the street. A tall man with a galumphing walk, stance, manner. A squirt of coffee. A squirt of cream. Purple handle on the carafe means half-and-half. Coffee cup not yet full.

A dash of Splenda. Two more squirts of coffee. A taste-test. One more squirt of half-and-half. the Pilgrim watches, feels like a primatologist observing a baboon in an onscreen jungle.

When he gets his brew just right, the bus-driver pivots, sees the Pilgrim waiting at double social distance, almost nods, catches himself—no need to apologize for one's anal habits during the last downhill phase of Covid. The bus driver pauses at the customer self-check do-it-yourself station. That simple move gives him one-up on the Pilgrim, who shows his age infirmity by paying cash-money to a real-live checker.

One day, if management has its way, there will be no checkers.

No stockers of shelves.

No humans behind the deli counter.

No butchers cutting meat.

No swampers sweeping the floor.

And the Pilgrim, with his machine-delivered coffee, will be forced to master the payout machine, using a credit card. No cash allowed.

What is cash?

❊ ❊ ❊

The narrow southside parking lot at the PCC looks across 65th to a Bryant Park greensward. Play swings for kids, iron bars and a sand-box. A covered table. A trash can. Two basketball hoops. And two sunken tennis courts.

Court One is reservable. Just call Amy Yee and pay your $15. And Court Two is open, with more puddles made more dangerous by largish trees dropping needles on the back of the court.

Before he climbs behind the wheel of his Rav4, the Pilgrim shoots an i-phone photo of the courts, a reminder to Players JD and PH so that they won't forget to bring squeegee and towels to the weekly Friday workout.

The Threesome of Bryant Park.

The quick and deadly way to end his Pilgrimage and his life is to get slammed crossing 65th, scooting out of the PCC parking lot, waiting, waiting, waiting—aware of the headlights behind him, drivers nosing up from behind, they want out, and then darting across at a diagonal, zooming across the westbound lane and joining the traffic on the east-bound lane.

No crunch of metal and bone.

Okay.

He does it again.

Now the pilgrim is headed east by south-east, climbing a curious hill that becomes a major hill near the top.

Vehicles whoosh by. The Pilgrim sips his coffee. Loud orange signs announce Men At Work up ahead. A City bus coming off the horseshoe curve between Ann Arbor, Princeton and 50th gobbles up the road, rolling out onto 65th as the Pilgrim rounds the hill.

If you check a city map, this bump in the road plots a half-circle around half a secluded glen, smell of old money, early city-settlers building on this high-point for the view, these bastionistic castles re-routing a major arterial, fouling the edgy traffic-laden straight-arrow progress of the pilgrim on his way to the Cathedral of Tennis.

65th Street breaks here, curves around to the south, steeper on the upside of the hill, signs bidding drivers to slow down—three battered cars parked on Princeton—fenders stripped away, two flat tires, one smashed windshield—because they forgot to heed the yellow slow signs—and now awaiting help from down below.

65th Street picks up again on the east side of this dangerous and exclusive enclave, at 51st, where the Pilgrim is never surprised to see a flagman waving his flag, while workers in orange vests bend to their task—keeping the arterial usable for trucks and city busses and drivers in pricey cars who rush to clog the pilgrim's progress to his own ritualized visit.

The Pilgrim's journey becomes more complicated as he approaches the crossing for the Burke-Gilman Trail. A stop sign says stop. Three speedy motorists in front of the Pilgrim wait for two bikers and a runner made invisible by his costume of total black.

On bright sunny mornings, the jagged shadows obscure runners and bikers and skaters, forcing drivers to crawl across this complex barricade, only to be edged out by the concrete wall of a dedicated bike lane that runs along the south side of 65th— the same concrete wall that forces the Pilgrim to crawl his way eastward to the stoplight on Sandpoint Way.

Autos and trucks.

Runners and moms pushing prams.

A senior player in a Warm-Up Suit carrying her racket in a rucksack slung across her back trots across the road.

Too fast for the Pilgrim to offer a ride.

But he does remember seeing her name on the roster for Complimentary Senior Doubles.

The pilgrim checks his chronometer.

The time is 7:52.

Play begins at 8:15.

Today's pilgrimage from the Pilgrim's hut in Olympic Manor clocks out at 24 minutes.

The pathway to the Cathedral leads the Pilgrim eastbound across Sand Point Way, down the hill to Sportsfield Drive, left turn, the excitement starting to build.

A combination of hope and fear.

Will he have the serve today?

Will he have the forehand slice?

Will he nail just one accursed high ball?

Sportsfield Drive curves past a covey of birds.

The speed limit is 20 MPH.

Three sets of headlights slashing through his rear window urge the Pilgrim to speed it up.

Burn more gas.

Fill the soft, moist air with fumes.

Life is short. Fill up the sky.

Take lots of vacations.

Drive in from the suburbs.

Burn more fossil fuel.
Speed up global warming.
The pathway curves.
Madison Park 6 on the right.
Through the windshield, the Pilgrim's first look at the TCSP, his chosen Cathedral of Tennis.
Seven years back, he was a stranger.
They took him in.
Seven years of tennis times 3 pilgrimages a week minus off-days for snow and sleet and bellyaches and ankles and knees and time spent out of town.
Equals 900 pilgrimages.
Plus or minus.
Enough repetition to establish the pilgrimage as a ritual.

* * *

The Pilgrim enters the building. He's on his way to the Men's Room, his private stall, with the extra high commode to qualify it as mandated for Old People.
The toilet is essential to the Pilgrim's ritual pilgrimage. The door locks. The outer door opens. The Pilgrim squats, listening.
A raspy cough.
Triggering fears of Covid.
Safe inside his stall, the Pilgrim experiences success.
Smiles as he cleans up.
Signs of life abounding.
The Pilgrim grunts as he tightens his belt.
The Pilgrim's rituals—journey, warm-up, Men's Room—secure his space inside his own personal tennis bubble.
The repetition helps him feel secure.
The ritual of playing tennis three times a week allows him to face up to his weaknesses.
Allows him to win the occasional point.
Allows him to hit one more ball.

Allows him to admire his spin-ball handiwork made possible by the cool tennis court under the unwinking lights set in the ceiling of his own Cathedral of Sport, Tennis Center Sand Point.

Has the final Pilgrimage happened?

Is this the summation of a life devoted to tennis?

The Pilgrim thrusts himself through the slit in the green tarp, where his tennis friends from SD&P are waiting.

As he begins warming up, finding the ball with his strings, the Pilgrim feels a burst of silvery sadness.

The ball curves itself across the net
If it must end
Then allow it to end here
On this blue-green court
Still swinging
Feeling the ball on his strings
One more time

OFF-COURT READING TO ENHANCE YOUR ON-COURT ACTIVITY

Every senior tennis player should read *Match Play and the Spin of the Ball*, by William T. Tilden (1925)—written before he went to jail for sexual abuse—and full of tennis savvy: "Let me suggest the ball for a moment as an individual. It is a third party in a match. Will this third party be on your side or against you?"

(Translation: control of the ball comes with spin; get friendly with spin.)

Follow Tilden's *Match Play* with Frank Deford's biography, *Big Bill Tilden: The Triumphs and the Tragedy*. A sad tale of the downfall of a tennis genius.

Deford also helped Arthur Ashe write *Arthur Ashe: Portrait in Motion*, where Ashe paints memorable portraits of tennis people on the tour: Stan Smith, Bob Lutz, Bud Collins, Ile Nastase, Jan Kodes.

Ashe was smart and brave and tactical and well-educated, with a keen eye for tennis talent—the guys who could beat him, the guys he could beat.

Ashe's mythic tennis strokes prompted New Yorker writer John McPhee to conjure up *Levels of the Game*, with precision prose that bears re-reading: "Ashe is a master of drop shots, of drop half volleys, of miscellaneous dinks and chips. He is, in the idiom of the game, very tough at cat-and-mouse."

The core of McFee's book is a match between Arthur Ashe and Clark Graebner, Forest Hills, 1968. Between points, McFee threads the reader into back story, charting the paths of both players (one black, one white) to the U.S. Open, when it was still played on East Coast grass, before the construction of the Arthur Ashe Stadium.

If you crave John McFee's exacting prose style with photos, check out *Wimbledon: A Celebration*, which opens with one of those terse McFee scene-setters: "Hoad on Court 5."

The best-written book on tennis history from the 1960s and 70s (Senior netsters lived those glory days—oh nostalgia!) is *Game, Set and Match*, by Herbert Warren Wind, who gained his fame writing about golf.

Wind's precise prose style will slow down your reading, but if you're in a hurry, then you can rush through *As Tom Goes By*, by Tom Brown, a fellow senior player who had his knees replaced (pause for a senior tennis moment) and was still playing into his 80's. In his thirties and forties, Brown was ranked in the U.S. top 10 eight times between 1946 and 1958. He played Davis Cup three times. In 1946 he held a US ranking of number 3.

In this memoir controlled by the white male First Person pronoun "I", Brown fails to mention Arthur Ashe. He fails to mention Althea Gibson.

There are some good-fun backstage stories about major tennis stars who get prose-style help from savvy ghost-writers. For *Open*, Andre Agassi hired a professional journalist, J. R. Moehringer. The best part of this book comes early, when Agassi reveals his merciless childhood training—which is a clue to his godlike reflexes, timing, and eyesight.

Martina Navratilova's book, called *Martina*, covers her defection—she left her native Czechoslovakia behind, took refuge in the U.S., and didn't see her mother for four years. The writing, helped by George Vecsey, sportswriter for the NYT, makes for easy, breezy reading. Martina is in top form when she comments on tennis matches for the Tennis Channel, showing off her command of English and her super-star-level understanding of the game of tennis at the pro-level.

Amazing woman. A brilliant Tennis Brain.

Billie Jean King's *All In: An Autobiography*, opens with an essay on injustice and exclusion, setting up her big-time tennis career, which began with free tennis lessons in the neighborhood park, in Long Beach—she wanted to play baseball, but there was no women's league, so she played tennis. Her version of the 1973 match with Bobby Riggs, made into a TV movie called "Battle of the Sexes," is a must read. In her thirties, when King was slowing down, she got some advice from Rod Laver, who was five years older: "Billie," Laver said. "You'll find that when you're out hitting some days, you just want to hit one ball—one ball that feels like it did in the old days."

The Match: Althea Gibson and Angela Buxton, by Bruce Schoenfeld, is a study in the systematic exclusion of two women players by the white tennis establishment. Gibson was black. Buxton was Jewish. They were both tough. They met in New Delhi in 1955. They won the women's doubles trophy at Wimbledon in 1956. They were both ostracized, shunted to the sidelines in the corridors of world tennis. They were both coached by men who were also ostracized. Gibson's coach, Sidney Llewellyn, brightened her future by changing her forehand grip from Continental to Eastern. She'd been winning with power. After the grip change, she won by aiming her shots.

String Theory, by David Foster Wallace, who grew up playing tennis in the wild winds of Illinois, land of tornadoes and tilted tennis courts, shares with the world a deep look at a professional tennis player in his essay on Michael Joyce (then ranked seventy-ninth in the world), warming up in Montreal—Foster Wallace uses Joyce to alert tennis fans who watch tennis on TV—about the distorted slowing down of the speed and power of tennis at the pro level—and then launches into a useful meditation on pro-tennis vs. the amateur game (this guy can really write):

"I still consider myself an extremely good tennis player, real hard to beat. Before coming to Montreal, I'd seen professional tennis only on television, which as has been noted does not give the viewer a very accurate picture of how good pros are on TV (while eating junk and smoking) I'd seen pros whacking the balls at each other that didn't look to be substantially faster than the balls I hit.

"…pros simply do not make unforced errors—or at any rate they make them so rarely that there's no way they're going to make the four unforced errors in seven points necessary for me to win a game…their own shots have such ferocious depth and pace that there's no way I'd be able to hit more than a couple of them back at any one time. I could not meaningfully exist on the same court with these obscure hungry players. Nor could you."

The book every senior should read is *Strokes of Genius: Federer, Nadal, and the Greatest Match Ever Played*, by L. Jon Wertheim. A deep probing insight-heavy look into the athletic gifts of Federer and Nadal in the 2008 Wimbledon Final, the Fed on the way down, Rafa on the way up, by a Tennis Channel commentator. How can you go wrong with prose like this, describing Nadal's white tank top: "It was made of a wicking microfiber that served the dual function of displacing his copious sweat and accentuating his propane-tank biceps."

Seniors might live longer and play better if they read *The Best Tennis of Your Life*, where author Jeff Greenwald unclogs your ego by nailing down your level of intensity: "…practice using a numbering system from 1 to 10, with 10 being the most intense for you and 1 being the most passive. Once you find your ideal level (most players choose between 7 and 10), you can then practice hitting the ball at this ideal level and checking in with your body, drills, or rallies.…"

GO!

Senior Tennis: Strokes, Strategies, Rules and Remedies, by George Wachtel, with a Foreword by Roy Emerson, is packed with advice for seniors: how to handle the underhand serve; how to survive a moon-baller; how to stay in shape. If your opponents are big tall men, hit the ball right at them. Take away their reach. Photos. Quotes and quips. The author's exercise routine shows discipline in action. Most of the tennis tales involve players rated 4.0 and above.

How to Play Winning Doubles. By George Lott and Jeffrey Bairstow, illustrations by Laura Duggan. Lott focuses on three shots: the forehand drive, the lob, and the chip—"each of which must be hit with almost the same motion to achieve maximum effect." Seniors can learn a ton from the diagrams.

GIVING THANKS

Writers write the words, but friends and helpers and spouses shape the writing. They drive the story.

My wife Margot kept me going with three words: "Hit Those Keys!" She brought food. We drank wine together. She asked how it was going. No book can be done without her.

Jack Remick—writer, co-author, critic, poet, fellow-teacher, friend—read every word more than once. Then helped me navigate into Kindle Create.

After reading the manuscript, Meredith Bricken Mills offered excellent advice on tone and then gifted me with the cover.

Paul Haley drew the tiny courts, the tiny nets, the lines of flight, the little old people doing drills. When I had to miss a session of SD&P (Senior Drill and Play), Paul's jolly e-mails kept me up to speed. Driven by the demon of simplicity, he persuaded me to change "racquet" to "racket." Paul shot the photo that Meredith used for the cover—"Author in Full Flight."

Živa Gronostalski showed me how to survive in Cyberspace. She built my website and helped with formatting and publishing.

Aki Carroll did a brilliant job of proof-reading. If errors on the page remain, blame them on me.

Zack Hoffman got me back on the court after a two-decade absence.

Jeanette Dassel fortified the Bryant Park Threesome with sweet treats.

Mark Ball, the ubiquitous Coach MB, kept me in learning mode for a glorious decade. I have worked with—and taken lessons from—more than 50 tennis coaches—Mark Ball is the best.

Johann Tan, my first instructor (Ball Machine), kept me stabilized on the court with these words: "Bobbie Ray, you've played this game before."

Thanks to the Royal Tennis Writers, Tony G, Mike E, Zack H, Barbara G, Joyce J, Ruthann M, Lorie P, Dr. Bob S, Dr. Mark S—for sharing their prose. Without you guys, this book would not have been possible.

ABOUT THE AUTHOR

Robert J. Ray

I am married to Margot—a terrific wife—she urges me to keep playing. We live in Seattle, where I am lucky to play at a club called TCSP, Tennis Center Sand Point.

Robert J. Ray is the author of 17 books. A detective series set in San Diego starring Matt Murdock, private eye. Small Business: An Entrepreneur's Plan, a textbook on starting your own small business—went through multiple editions. Three Weekend Novelist books, one co-authored by Jack Remick. A "big book" thriller that the publisher squeezed down, with tiny type, into a chubby paperback. Ray's first book—The Art of Reading: A Handbook on Writing—helped countless students read deeper, which caused them to write better. Play or Die is his first plunge into the mystery of memoir.

Read more at https://robertjraywrites.com/

BOOKS BY THIS AUTHOR

The Weekend Novelist

During the week Robert J. Ray was a teacher. On weekends he learned the fiction writer's craft and produced his first novel. He ended up selling six books in six years. The same success as a writer can happen to you.

The Weekend Novelist Writes A Mystery

Like Agatha Christie and Raymond Chandler, Sara Paretsky and Thomas Harris, you, too, can learn the trade secrets of quality detective fiction.

The Weekend Novelist Rewrites The Novel

You've finished your first draft—congratulations! Think it's ready for publication? Think again. The next stage is all about revising and reworking your manuscript—fine-tuning the plot, adding or improving subplots, and fleshing out characters; in short, addressing important structural issues that make or break a novel.

Bloody Murdock (A Matt Murdock Murder Mystery: Book 1)

Ex-cop turned PI Matt Murdock reluctantly takes on a bodyguard case involving a high-handed client and the puzzling death of a beautiful woman, leading to a tangled web of secrets and danger as they discover just how dirty deals in Hollywood can get.

Murdock Cracks Ice (A Matt Murdock Murder Mystery: Book 2)

A deadly killer has iced Rollie Nielsen, a smart college kid with a brain for chemistry, and his dad wants to know why. Private investigator Matt Murdock is hired to uncover the truth and discovers Rollie was involved in a dangerous drug lab. As he navigates a treacherous path filled with enemies and secrets, Murdock seeks to unearth Rollie's lab with the help of a sexy female acquaintance of Rollie's and wannabe detective, Louie Chen, all while staying one step ahead of Seattle's most powerful drug kingpin.

Murdock For Hire (A Matt Murdock Murder Mystery: Book 3)

When software mogul Eddie Hennessy's death raises suspicion due to the family man's involvement with a masked call-girl and cocaine, private-eye Matt Murdock gets involved to help the widow find Eddie's missing coin collection. He uncovers a high-class escort service targeting stressed-out businessmen, holding their reputations for ransom. Can Murdock infiltrate their inner sanctum and break their hold on Newport Beach's corporate class? Sure, but not without stirring up a hornets' nest that threatens to take out both Murdock and his shady lady love.

Merry Christmas, Murdock (A Matt Murdock Murder Mystery: Book 4)

Private-eye Matt Murdock gets entangled in a Christmastime mystery involving a missing author, a comatose teenager, and a hit-and-run investigation, all while navigating the complicated dynamics of wealthy families and figuring out how to romance the lovely senator, Jane Blasingame.

Dial "M" For Murdock (A Matt Murdock Murder Mystery: Book 5)

Insurance investigator Bruce Halliburton hires private-eye Matt Murdock to look into a suspected faked death but when he ends up dead himself, that just leaves Roxanne, the lovely widow whose husband, Emiliano Mendez-Madrid, died of a heart attack after insuring his life ten times over. Roxanne hires Matt to find the money and keep her safe. Now he smells trouble. If he falls too hard for the widow and connects all the dots, he might just end up decorated with a line of lead like his old pal Bruce.

Murdock Tackles Taos (A Matt Murdock Murder Mystery: Book 6)

Weary private-eye Matt Murdock and writer/cop's daughter Helene Steinbeck join forces to search for a missing friend's daughter, but their investigation unveils a dangerous cult with powerful allies in Taos. As Helene becomes both Murdock's apprentice and lover, they must outwit numerous adversaries to uncover the truth.

Murdock Rocks Sedona (Matt Murdock Murder Mystery: Book 7)

Wealthy investors in Sedona, Arizona, are mysteriously meeting fatal accidents, all linked to their involvement with Sedona Landing, a hotel owned by billionaire Axel Ackerman. Ackerman hires investigators Matt Murdock and Helene Steinbeck to uncover the personal vendetta behind these incidents in "Murdock Rocks Sedona,"

Made in the USA
Columbia, SC
25 September 2023